GW00670457

Yorkshire Dales

Walks

Compiled by
Terry Marsh

Contents

At-a-glance

Walk		Page	🖌		🗻	🏁	⛰	🕐
1	Richmond and Easby	10	Richmond	NZ 168 011	3¾ miles (6km)	460ft (140m)	2 hrs
2	Hawes and Hardraw Force	12	Hawes	SD 875 898	4 miles (6.5km)	510ft (155m)	2 hrs
3	Ingleton Waterfalls	14	Ingleton	SD 693 733	4 miles (6.5km)	1,035ft (315m)	2½ hrs
4	How Stean Gorge and Upper Nidderdale	16	Lofthouse	SE 101 735	4¼ miles (7km)	670ft (205m)	2½ hrs
5	Grassington and the River Wharfe	18	Grassington	SE 002 637	5 miles (8km)	655ft (200m)	2½ hrs
6	West Burton	20	Aysgarth	SE 011 884	5¼ miles (8.5km)	690ft (210m)	2½ hrs
7	Sulber Nick	24	Horton-in-Ribblesdale	SD 807 726	5½ miles (8.75km)	720ft (220m)	3 hrs
8	Reeth, Arkengarthdale and Grinton	26	Reeth	SE 038 993	5½ miles (8.7km)	540ft (165m)	3 hrs
9	Aysgarth Falls and Bolton Castle	29	Aysgarth Falls	SE 012 887	6 miles (9.9km)	575ft (175m)	3 hrs
10	Dentdale	32	Dent	SD 704 871	6 miles (9.5km)	920ft (280m)	3 hrs
11	Cam Head	34	Kettlewell	SD 968 723	6 miles (9.6km)	1,180ft (360m)	3½ hrs
12	Kettlewell and Arncliffe	36	Kettlewell	SD 968 723	6 miles (9.8km)	1,590ft (485m)	3½ hrs
13	Burnsall and Linton	38	Burnsall	SE 031 611	6½ miles (10.5km)	740ft (225m)	3½ hrs
14	Ribblehead and Chapel-le-Dale	41	Ribblehead	SD 764 791	6¾ miles (11km)	605ft (185m)	3½ hrs
15	Burnsall, Trollers Gill and Appletreewick	44	Burnsall	SE 031 611	7 miles (11.2km)	835ft (255m)	3½ hrs
16	Clapham, Crummack Dale and Austwick	47	Clapham	SD 745 692	6¾ miles (11km)	785ft (240m)	3½ hrs
17	Around Malham	50	Malham	SD 900 627	7 miles (11.5km)	920ft (280m)	3½ hrs
18	Buckden and Langstrothdale Chase	55	Buckden	SD 942 774	7 miles (11.2km)	920ft (280m)	3½ hrs
19	Pen-y-ghent	58	Horton-in-Ribblesdale	SD 807 726	6 miles (9.5km)	1,610ft (490m)	3½ hrs
20	Sedbergh and Winder	62	Sedbergh	SD 658 920	7 miles (11.5km)	1,445ft (440m)	4 hrs
21	Bolton Abbey, Barden Tower and The Strid	65	Bolton Abbey	SE 071 539	7½ miles (12km)	1,035ft (315m)	4 hrs
22	Giggleswick Scar and Stainforth Force	68	Settle	SD 819 638	8½ miles (13.5km)	1,245ft (380m)	4½ hrs
23	Semer Water	71	Bainbridge	SD 934 902	8½ miles (13.5km)	1,395ft (425m)	4½ hrs
24	Pateley Bridge and Brimham Rocks	74	Pateley Bridge	SE 157 655	9 miles (14.5km)	1,245ft (380m)	4½ hrs
25	Ingleborough from Ingleton	78	Ingleton	SD 695 730	8 miles (13km)	2,035ft (620m)	5 hrs
26	Nine Standards Rigg	81	Kirkby Stephen	NY 775 087	9 miles (14.5km)	1,770ft (540m)	5 hrs
27	Ingleborough from Clapham	85	Clapham	SD 745 692	10½ miles (17km)	2,230ft (680m)	5½ hrs
28	Gunnerside, Kisdon and Muker	89	Gunnerside	SD 951 982	11¼ miles (18km)	1,790ft (545m)	6 hrs

Comments

A short walk from the historical town of Richmond that visits a medieval abbey, riverside paths and the trackbed of the former valley railway.

Providing fine views across Wensleydale, this walk also takes in the highest single drop waterfall in the Dales, accessed, conveniently some might say, through a pub.

Delightfully wooded rocky gorges provide the setting for the two main arms of this walk, linked by a trek across hill slopes with lovely views. *The paths can be very slippery when wet or icy.*

This splendid walk first visits the dramatic How Stean Gorge before sauntering up-dale to explore the course of the River Nidd.

Limestone moorland, woodland and the company of the River Wharfe make this a memorable walk for all seasons.

Beginning alongside the River Ure with its spectacular falls, the walk then climbs to a hillside chapel before trekking along a splendid grassy ridge to the village of West Burton.

A splendid exploration of extensive limestone pavement with interesting flora, and views over the Ribble Valley to Pen-y-Ghent. Some fascinating geology and long lost streams.

An opportunity to explore Arkengarthdale, the most northerly of the Yorkshire Dales before returning in a wide loop that visits Grinton, an ancient and once important centre for the dale.

Apart from wandering some delectable countryside, the main interests in this walk lie in the spectacular waterfalls and the dominating presence of Bolton Castle.

Dentdale is different from most of the dales, with hedgerows, not walls, separating the pastures. This walk begins up a wooded ravine, takes in a stroll above the valley and concludes in the company of the river.

A steady climb above Wharfedale from the village of Kettlewell, the walk enjoys fine views and concludes along a section of the Dales Way beside the River Wharfe.

The initial ascent from Kettlewell is well worth the effort and rewards with delightful views. Arncliffe is a gem of a village, and the company of the Skirfare is of the highest order.

Starting along the river, this walk visits some stunning scenery and an isolated village before returning at a high level across undulating pastures with excellent views of the dale.

Sandwiched between two of Yorkshire's 'Three Peaks' this walk makes the most of the pastoral countryside and visits the outstanding Ribblehead viaduct.

This walk combines attractive villages, open moorland, a steep-sided ravine and riverside pastures; there is also the option to visit the grounds of an outstanding 17th-century hall.

A fascinating encounter with glacial rubbish leads into a wild and remote dale before returning along a walled lane to the village of Austwick.

Waterfalls, limestone gorges and the magnificence of Malham Cove combine to make this an outstanding walk, one of the finest in England.

A high level outward route with superb views of Upper Wharfedale is followed by a lovely return stretch by the river, and visiting the hamlet of Hubberholme.

A popular walk to a very distinctive summit, with an option to visit a magnificent pot hole on the way up. Part of the route follows the Pennine Way. *The initial descent is steep and rocky.*

The sleek, grassy fellsides of the Howgills provide a grand introduction to this circular tour at the north-western edge of the National Park.

This walk begins across moorland pasture before descending to savour one of the most delectable stretches of the River Wharfe on its return to the ruins of Bolton Priory.

Offering a stunning introduction to limestone escarpment and plateaux, this walk also has outstanding views of Ribblesdale, before experiencing the thrill of a fine cascade and concluding along a riverside path.

Visiting a lonely lake with a grim tale to tell, the walk later climbs high onto moors across which the Romans built one of their major roads.

The highlight of this walk is unquestionably Brimham Rocks, a collection of weirdly fashioned grit-stone boulders, but there is much more to the walk, which is best reserved for a fine day.

A dramatic way onto Ingleborough, beginning easily enough, but later with the summit full in your face, as you plod across superb moorland, and climb through layers of geology.

Follow the Coast-to-Coast walk to a fine vantage point on the watershed of Britain and the gathering grounds of the River Swale; *an optional extension explores boggy moorland where navigational skills are vital.*

A long but delightful walk to a superb summit with excellent views, and a chance to visit one of England's most famous pot holes.

A delightfully varied walk taking both high and low level views of Swaledale, and passing riverside meadows, moorland fringes, waterfalls and woodland.

Keymap

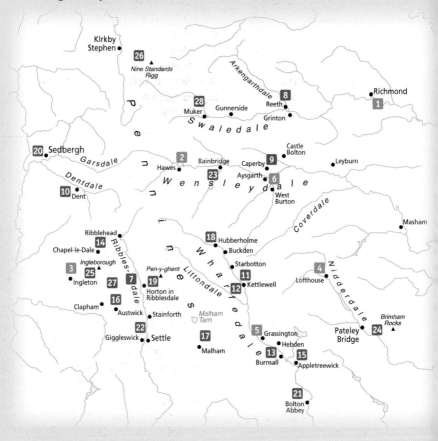

Introduction to the Yorkshire Dales

An alternative name for the Yorkshire Dales could be the Middle Pennines. To the north, extending through Cumbria, Durham and Northumberland, lies the wild and remote country of the North Pennines, while to the south, eventually merging almost imperceptibly with the Peak District, are the bare gritstone moorlands of the South Pennines. The most distinctive feature of the Yorkshire Dales, which lie between them, is the magnificent limestone landscape that encompasses a major proportion of the area, and around which the National Park is largely based.

Within that area is some of the most attractive countryside in Britain, offering infinite enjoyment and variety to those who are prepared to explore on foot. On the high, exposed moorlands, often buffeted by wind and rain, lonely, austere and dramatic countryside will be found. The valleys, however, present a striking contrast: a gentle scene with small woods, riverside meadows and neat green fields separated by miles of drystone walls, dotted with exquisite and unspoilt villages whose welcoming pubs and tearooms offer relaxation and sustenance.

It is chiefly the upper and middle reaches of the valleys of the Ribble, Aire, Wharfe, Nidd, Ure and Swale, together with their tributaries and the land between them, that form the Yorkshire Dales. The unique landscape of the region has been fashioned by the combined forces of nature and man over an immensely long time.

The forces of nature

Millions of years ago, massive earth movements thrust the Pennines above the surrounding area and also created the series of fractures called the Craven Faults. Here the rocks on one side of the fault have been lifted high above those on the other side, which have been displaced and buried thousands of feet below. This phenomenon is best observed on Giggleswick Scar, where the line of the fault is followed by the main road from Settle to Kendal. Later, during the ice age, huge glaciers flowed along the valleys, deepening and straightening them and smoothing their sides. As they moved, they dropped debris of different rocks at intervals, such as the Norber Erratics overlooking Crummack Dale, a large number of dark gritstone boulders perched above the surrounding plateau of white limestone. The scouring effect of the glaciers scraped clean and exposed expanses of bare rock, while torrents of meltwater from them were responsible for carving out most of the gorges in the area, such as Gordale Scar near Malham and Trow Gill near Clapham.

Limestone is the predominant rock throughout the Dales and this gives the area its most distinctive scenic features. This is especially true of the Craven area in the south, where the compacted Great Scar limestone comes close to the surface and exhibits all the features of 'karst' scenery, named after the Karst region of Slovenia, where similar geological features are found. Prominent among these features are the great expanses of exposed rock which gleam white in the sunlight, revealed in the vertical cliffs or 'scars' and the broad horizontal terraces or 'pavements'.

It is the action of water – either streams or rainwater – that produces most of the characteristics of limestone scenery. The water absorbs carbon dioxide from the atmosphere to form a weak acid solution, which slowly dissolves the limestone. The action of rainwater can be seen to good effect on the pavement above Malham Cove, the most visited of all the limestone pavements. Here rainwater has penetrated the cracks in the rock, slowly widening and deepening them to create an almost geometric pattern of blocks (called 'clints') separated by deep grooves or channels (called 'grikes').

Water finds its way through any joints in the rocks (called sink-holes), either seeping through gently or plunging down potholes (which are wider and deeper), such as the spectacular Gaping Gill on the lower slopes of Ingleborough, or Hull Pot near the base of Pen-y-ghent. This causes one of the most spectacular features of karst scenery: streams disappearing and flowing underground to leave dry valleys on the surface. As the water penetrates, it continues to dissolve the limestone, eventually creating a network of subterranean caverns, such as the 'show caves' near Ingleton and Clapham, and the Stump Cross Caverns between Grassington and Pateley Bridge.

Farther north, in Wensleydale

and Swaledale, the Yoredale series of rocks, called after the ancient name for Wensleydale, are dominant; alternating bands of coarse shales, limestone, sandstone and millstone grit. The differences between weaker and stronger rocks have created the many waterfalls found in this northern part of the dales. Millstone grit is the hardest and most weather resistant of all these rocks and, where the softer rocks have been worn away, areas of millstone grit remain, standing boldly above the surrounding landscape, either as the major outcrops that cap the summits of the 'Three Peaks' of Ingleborough, Pen-y-ghent and Whernside, or in the form of large groups of individual boulders, like the superb collection at Brimham Rocks overlooking Nidderdale. In the far north west, in the Cumbrian section of the dales, much older Silurian slates give rise to a landscape more typical of the highlands, with smooth, steep slopes bisected by deep ravines.

Man's influence

The Yorkshire Dales was never one of the more heavily populated areas of prehistoric Britain, and consequently remains of that period (stone circles and hillforts) are comparatively few and unimpressive. The Romans likewise left little mark on the area, but the line of a Roman road running from Ilkley to Bainbridge in Wensleydale, the principal Roman fort in the area, whose grassy ramparts still crown a hill above the village, can be traced for miles across the dales, and parts of it are now put to good purpose as a magnificent scenic footpath (see Walk 23).

Most of the settlements were originally founded during the Anglo-Saxon period, either by the Angles who settled in the region following the departure of the Romans, or by later Viking colonists, both Danish and Norse, from Scandinavia. The Danes penetrated into the area from the east coast, moving up the Humber and Ouse and across the Vale of York, while the Norsemen came from the west. A glance at a map reveals the intermingling of typical Anglo-Saxon place name endings (-ton, -ham, -den) with the Scandinavian endings (-by, -thorpe, -thwaite), and the predominance of Norse words, such as gill, beck, fell, crag and scar, describing physical features. The word 'dale' itself comes from a Danish word meaning 'valley'.

The Norman barons who accompanied William the Conqueror's successful expedition in 1066 founded churches, created hunting grounds, such as Lang-strothdale Chase in Upper Wharfedale, and, most notably, built castles at Skipton, Middleham and Richmond to secure their rule. In their wake came the monastic orders, especially the Cistercians, who were attracted to the comparatively remote and sparsely populated Yorkshire Dales because it provided them with the isolation that was an integral part of their code. Abbeys and priories arose on sheltered riverside sites at Bolton in Wharfedale, Jervaulx in Wensleydale, Coverham in Coverdale and Easby in Swaledale. Most imposing of all was Fountains Abbey, the most complete monastic ruin in Britain, which became the wealthiest of all Cistercian monasteries. The monks were great landowners and enterprising managers, clearing forests, improving drainage and developing a thriving sheep farming industry. Such entrepreneurial skills were to sow the seeds of their future downfall at the hands of Henry VIII in the 1530s.

Scottish raids were a continual threat in the later Middle Ages, which explains why residences continued to be built as fortified strongholds, as happened at Bolton Castle in Wensleydale and Barden Tower, just upstream from Bolton Abbey. After the monasteries were dissolved their extensive estates passed into new hands and this, coupled with the removal of the Scottish threat following the union of the crowns in 1603, led to a period of unprecedented prosperity in agriculture, reflected in the extensive rebuilding of farms and manor houses.

Looking around the area today it may come as a surprise to learn that the Yorkshire Dales has a long history as an industrial as well as a farming area. Lead mining was carried on for over 1,000 years, mainly in Swaledale but also in Nidderdale and Wharfedale, and only ceased in the early years of the 20th century. Quarrying, the other major industry, has continued to the present day.

Routes and transport

Before the construction of roads and railways, the main form of transport in the dales was by foot or on horseback, using the extensive network of 'green lanes', which are easily recognisable as broad, walled tracks. Nowadays they make excellent walking routes. Undoubtedly the most spectacular

Middle Force, at Aysgarth

transport undertaking in the dales was the Settle–Carlisle railway, built between 1869 and 1875 as a new alternative route between London and Scotland. It runs across some of the wildest and most inhospitable terrain in the country and its construction was a prodigious feat of Victorian civil engineering. Particularly impressive are the massive stone viaducts, such as Dent Head and Ribblehead, which stride across bleak and windswept countryside. Now, with the inevitable mellowing and acceptance that the passage of time brings, these appear to be almost part of the landscape, rather than the unwelcome and unsightly intrusions they seemed to be at first.

Plantations, reservoirs and tourists

The 20th century added at least two new features to the landscape, both of them controversial – conifer plantations and reservoirs, the latter mainly in Upper Nidderdale. But the major impact that the last century has had on the Yorkshire Dales is the growth of mass tourism.

The first tourists, apart from a few early intrepid explorers, were the Victorians, who came to view what they thought of as 'picturesque' sights: either natural wonders such as Malham Cove, Hardraw Force and Brimham Rocks, or the man-made, romantic-looking ruins of Bolton Priory and Fountains Abbey. Nowadays tourists flock into the area in ever increasing numbers for a wide variety of reasons, many of them of a recreational nature: rock climbing, potholing, canoeing, fishing, cycling or, most popular of all, walking.

The National Park

In 1954 most of the Yorkshire Dales area became one of the now thirteen National Parks of England and Wales. The boundaries were drawn to include, for obvious scenic and geographical reasons, a corner of south-eastern Cumbria, but Nidderdale was excluded, not, it must be emphasised, through any lack of scenic qualities, but because large parts of the upper dale were owned by water authorities and there were several reservoirs in the area.

The National Park Authority and the communities throughout the Dales welcome more and more visitors each year, but this does have an effect on the environment. To ensure that the landscape and the way of life of its inhabitants can be enjoyed in the future, it is important to treat the Dales gently. Where possible it is best to use public transport rather than your own car to reduce pollution and congestion of the environment. Information on local bus and train services can be found at any of the seven National Park visitor centres listed on pages 93-94. By supporting local services and businesses you will be benefiting not only the Dales communities but other visitors by ensuring that they remain open.

It is also important to understand the lifestyle in the Dales: treat the landscape with care and respect, trying not to disturb the wildlife. Remember that you may often find yourself on a path which crosses land that provides the livelihood for the local farming community, so consideration and common sense are needed to avoid unnecessary disruption and damage. It may be advisable to avoid certain moorland paths in winter or after a prolonged period of wet weather, or to follow any seasonal alternative routes provided to minimise the erosion of the walking paths.

Whether within the National Park boundaries or not, the varied and glorious scenery of the Yorkshire Dales is a paradise for walkers, offering everything from gentle lowland rambles which link attractive riverside villages, to more challenging and longer hikes across the moorland and ascents of some of the well-known peaks. The walks in this book embrace all these and illustrate both the scenic variety and the rich historic heritage of this region.

This book includes a list of waypoints alongside the description of the walk, so that you can enjoy the full benefits of gps should you wish to. For more information on using your gps, read the Pathfinder® Guide *GPS for Walkers*, by gps teacher and navigation trainer, Clive Thomas (ISBN 978-0-7117-4445-5). For essential information on map reading and basic navigation, read the Pathfinder® Guide *Map Reading Skills* by author of this title, Terry Marsh (ISBN 978-0-7117-4978-8). Both titles are available in bookshops or can be ordered online at www.totalwalking.co.uk

Thornton Force

Richmond and Easby

Start
Richmond

Distance
3¾ miles (6km)

Height gain
460 feet (140m)

Approximate time
2 hours

Route terrain
City streets and riverside paths

Parking
Car park on Victoria Road (Pay and Display)

OS maps
Landrangers 92 (Barnard Castle & Richmond) and 99 (Northallerton & Ripon), Explorer 304 (Darlington & Richmond)

GPS waypoints
NZ 168 011
Ⓐ NZ 175 010
Ⓑ NZ 185 002
Ⓒ SE 184 998
Ⓓ NZ 169 005

This easy half-day stroll begins in the centre of Richmond, a fascinating place to explore at the end of the walk. It is nowhere difficult, with good paths alongside and through riverside meadows, and always the delightful Swale for company. The remains of Easby Abbey add considerable interest to the walk, and are easily visited.

Richmond It is a most agreeable experience to explore the streets of Richmond, one of the great historic towns of England, a supremely attractive and photogenic old market town set beside the beautiful River Swale. Parts of the medieval walls still remain, along with the gateways and the narrow winding streets that characterise early town development. Elsewhere, there are elegant Georgian thoroughfares, a spacious if rather tilted market place, two medieval churches and the tower of a Franciscan friary. Of course, it is the great Norman castle, occupying a clifftop perch above the river and guarding the entrance to Swaledale, that so dominates the town. It was founded by Alan the Red of Brittany shortly after the Norman Conquest, and still retains part of the original 11th-century castle, known as Scotland's Hall, one of the earliest domestic buildings in the country. The remainder of the castle largely dates from the 12th century. Despite its size and air of impregnability, Richmond Castle's defences were never put to the test, and the castle enjoyed a rather peaceful existence.

For ease of parking, the walk begins from a car park along Victoria Road. From it, head eastwards along Victoria Road, passing playing fields on the left, to the junction with Queen's Road (the main road, which here bears left) and King Street. At this junction go forward to pass the **King's Head** pub and enter a narrow street, Ryders Wynd, which leads down to Frenchgate. Turn left and soon bear right into Station Road. Shortly before the road crosses the river, leave it by branching left into a side lane Ⓐ leading to a few houses, and there bear right onto a roughly surfaced lane that soon degenerates into a broad track.

Follow the track, which soon becomes a riverside path, leading eventually to a flight of steps up to a stile/gate giving into a field. Strike diagonally across the field, heading for another gate at the bottom end of a brief, sloping path leading above the grounds of Easby Abbey. Over a stile at the top of the path, bear right on a broad track to a road junction, and there turn right to walk down to a car park adjoining Easby Abbey **B**.

Continue past the car park, following a surfaced lane and track along the bottom edge of light woodland to reach a bridge adjoining a cottage **C**. Turn right over the bridge spanning the River Swale, now having encroached onto the trackbed of a former railway. This leads easily back to the old railway station, passing to the left of it to a road, and soon emerging on the main road not far from Station Bridge.

Walk to the bridge, and there go down steps to the riverbank, and then turn left under the bridge and along a riverside path once more. At the next bridge **D**, Richmond Bridge, turn right and walk up Bridge Street towards the centre of town. Turn right into Cornforth Hill and at a T-junction turn right again to reach the Market Place. Across the far side of Market Place is King Street, at the far end of which you meet Victoria Road. Turn left to return to the car park. ●

Easby Abbey

Easby Abbey occupies a tranquil position beside the River Swale, and apart from the occasional Scottish raid, like Richmond Castle seems to have enjoyed a peaceful existence. A house of Premonstratensian canons, it was founded in 1155, but like so many, came to an end in 1536 during Henry VIII's Dissolution of the Monasteries. The church is the least substantial surviving part, and of it only the presbytery remains, but there are extensive remains of the domestic buildings, notably the infirmary, dormitory and refectory. The inhabitants of the abbey were canons rather than monks, and so were able to serve the local population as parish priests.

SCALE 1:25000 or 2½ INCHES to 1 MILE 4CM to 1KM

0	200	400	600	800 METRES	1
					KILOMETRES
					MILES
0	200	400	600 YARDS	½	

Start

Hawes

Distance

4 miles (6.5km)

Height gain

510 feet (155m)

Approximate time

2 hours

Route terrain

Some road walking, limestone uplands

P **Parking**

Station Car Park (Pay and Display)

OS maps

Landranger 98 (Wensleydale & Upper Wharfedale), Explorer OL30 (Yorkshire Dales – Northern & Central areas)

GPS waypoints

SD 875 898
Ⓐ SD 876 907
Ⓑ SD 871 915
Ⓒ SD 882 911

Hawes and Hardraw Force

With the agreeable prospect of lunch in Hawes before or after the walk, this half-day excursion is a relaxing and pleasant introduction to Wensleydale. The walk includes a visit to Hardraw Force, the highest single fall in the Dales.

Hawes Hawes is a quaint arrangement of alleyways and cottages, concealed nooks and crannies, that give the impression of mellowed old age, but the town is only a mere youngster, unable to trace its pedigree beyond the 14th century. In fact, when the Domesday Book was compiled, Hawes and the countryside about was forest land, and, as Camden saw it, 'a dreary waste and horrid silent wilderness among the mountains...' The region, above and around the town, is still wild, but perceptions change and today the fellsides provide plenty of excuses to explore.

Begin from the corner of the car park on the site of the former railway and walk up a ramp to the road. Turn right to cross the railway line. Moves have long been afoot to re-open parts, of the railway line through Wensleydale, possibly as far as Garsdale, where it would link with the Settle–Carlisle line.

Take the first turning on the left, which goes into a small industrial estate, but immediately abandon that by passing through a gate onto a paved section of the Pennine Way, which heads across a field to re-emerge on the road near Hayland's Bridge.

Cross Hayland's Bridge, continuing along and up the road (*take care against approaching traffic*) as far as the signposted turning for Hardrow (sic) and the Pennine Way Ⓐ. Here leave the road, and go forward along a field-edge path. Continue by an obvious route across a series of fields to enter the village of Hardraw opposite the **Green Dragon Inn**.

Visitors wanting to see Hardraw Force must enter the pub and pay a small fee, as the waterfall is on private land. From the back of the inn, a path leads up into the amphitheatre into which Hardraw Beck plunges spectacularly.

Having visited the falls, turn around the end of the inn and through a gate and onto a footpath (signposted for Simonstone), which passes a cottage then soon starts heading up a field to a step-stile. Nearby, in the wall on the left, is a small mosaic, one

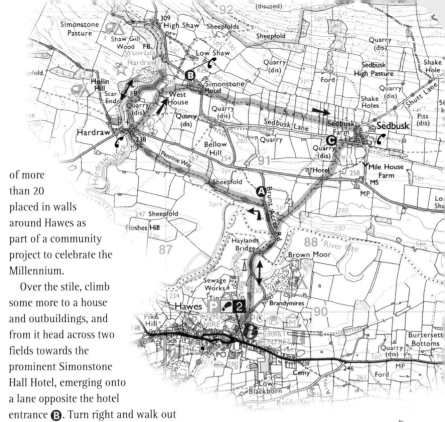

of more than 20 placed in walls around Hawes as part of a community project to celebrate the Millennium.

Over the stile, climb some more to a house and outbuildings, and from it head across two fields towards the prominent Simonstone Hall Hotel, emerging onto a lane opposite the hotel entrance **B**. Turn right and walk out to a T-junction. Go left to a signposted stile on the right giving onto a footpath for Sedbusk. Initially the path goes forward as a broad track towards farm buildings, beyond which cross a ladder-stile and then pursue an obvious route across a succession of fields linked by gated gap-stiles.

Eventually, the ongoing path emerges into the hamlet of Sedbusk, opposite a telephone box. Turn right and walk

down to a junction near a post box in a wall, and here turn right along a narrow lane, passing Rose Cottage. After about 165 yds, leave the lane at a signposted path on the left **C** for Hayland's Bridge. Go through a gap-stile and downfield, to the right of a barn and across to another stile beyond.

The gated route leads to a road, cross this and go through another stile. In the ensuing pasture a clear, grassy path leads across to Hayland's Bridge. The path first crosses a stream by a footbridge before continuing out to meet the road. Turn left and retrace the outward route back to Hawes. ●

SCALE 1:25000 or 2½ INCHES to 1 MILE 4CM to 1KM

Meadowland and field barn, Hardraw

Ingleton Waterfalls

Start

Ingleton

Distance

4 miles (6.5km)

Height gain

1,035 feet (315m)

Approximate time

2½ hours

Route terrain

Woodland; farmland; riverside paths and steps

P Parking

At start (Fee for parking and admission to waterfalls – trail open daily from 09.00 to dusk)

Dog friendly

All bridges (4) have open mesh underfoot, and this can be disconcerting for some dogs

OS maps

Landranger 98 (Wensleydale & Upper Wharfedale), Explorer OL2 (Yorkshire Dales – Southern & Western areas)

GPS waypoints

SD 693 733
Ⓐ SD 695 750
Ⓑ SD 701 751
Ⓒ SD 705 747

This is an 'up, across and down' walk: 'up' the narrow gorge of the River Twiss; 'across' a stretch of open countryside on an ancient track, and 'down' the spectacular gorge of the River Doe. It is attractive whatever the time of year, but although the paths are clear and well maintained, the rocks can be slippery when wet (as they often are), and care is needed in winter if ice lies on the steps. Although a short walk, there is much to see, and quite a lot of clambering up and down. Because most of the walk is on private land, there is a charge for visitors, which includes parking.

Ingleton is a delightful, homely place, dominated by a huge Victorian railway viaduct, now redundant, but formerly the route by which many visitors came to the area. Tourists still arrive in their droves, making this walk one of the most popular in the Dales. *(NOTE: If you intend to undertake this walk, bear in mind that if you park in the village centre (Station) car park, you will have to pay there, and again as you set off on the walk.)*

Begin from the parking area at the foot of Swilla Glen. There is a **café** here (open all year), and just beyond it a kiosk where you pay your admission fee and go on to park. (Be sure to hold on to your tickets all day, in order to retrieve your car.) On the far side of the parking area, continue along a broad track that soon narrows to a path through light oak woodland with crags above, and following the course of the Twiss. A gate marks the start of Swilla Glen, a steep-sided, narrow ravine, bright with flowers and ferns, and loud with birdsong. Keep an eye open for a 'Money Tree', especially those readers who do not believe that money grows on trees. There are more, later in the walk.

Onward there is no choice of route, a clear path leading to a footbridge spanning the river and climbing a little to a viewpoint from which you get a first glimpse of the impressive Pecca Falls upstream. Another bridge takes you back across the river before reaching the falls, and the path climbs beside them offering splendid views. With white water a constant companion you now climb further to a gate beyond which there is a seasonal snack bar Ⓐ, which also doubles as a ticket sales point for anyone undertaking the walk in the opposite direction.

Press on past the kiosk, and soon the path levels as you approach a neat amphitheatre into which Thornton Force plunges with considerable force.

Climb, left, past the falls to gain a more tranquil area, where the river is much more calm and sedate, and the valley sides fall back and relax to reveal Kingsdale, through which the River Twiss is formed, and the slopes of Gragareth, the long ridge leading up to Green Hill, at 628m (2,060ft), the highest top in Lancashire. A short way on, another footbridge leads to steps by which you finally climb out of the gorge to a gate giving on to an ancient walled track cutting across the landscape below Twistleton Scar End.

Turn right and follow the track as far as a farm **B** at Twistleton Hall. Keep left to pass the farm, beyond which the ongoing track (signed for Beezley Falls) leads through a field gate and down to intercept a surfaced lane (Oddie's Lane). Now entering the valley of the River Doe, cross the lane and go down a surfaced track opposite that leads to another farmhouse. Here swing right and soon reach a seasonal **Refreshment Centre** and ticket kiosk.

Continue descending, gently, to a gate giving into the wooded gorge of the Doe **C**. Now more waterfalls appear, beginning immediately with Beezley Falls. The ongoing path twists and turns, climbs and falls, but is never in doubt and provides a truly special experience as you steadily descend through the gorge: Rival Falls, Baxenghyll Gorge and Snow Falls, all provide interest and entertainment. A footbridge (do not be drawn by an earlier one that crosses the river into closed mining shafts) leads across to the

true left bank of the Doe, after which the gorge opens out and becomes less steep-sided with much evidence of quarrying hereabouts.

Soon Ingleton appears ahead, and the path broadens into a rough track that leads out to a gate, beyond which a surfaced lane takes you to the village. At the main street, turn right to pass the church and take a road descending on the right to cross the River Twiss, shortly after which you can turn right to complete the walk. ●

🖊 Start
Lofthouse

➤ Distance
4¼ miles (7km)

⛰ Height gain
670 feet (205m)

🕐 Approximate time
2½ hours

👢 Route terrain
Riverside paths, farmland, some road walking

P Parking
Limited parking in Lofthouse, or use How Stean car park

🧭 OS maps
Landranger 99 (Northallerton & Ripon), Explorer OL30 (Yorkshire Dales – Northern & Central areas)

📱 GPS waypoints
🖊 SE 101 735
Ⓐ SE 088 735
Ⓑ SE 092 743
Ⓒ SE 095 755
Ⓓ SE 099 758

How Stean Gorge and Upper Nidderdale

How Stean Beck makes an impressive display as it bullies its way through a narrow gorge bound for the River Nidd, which it joins below the village of Lofthouse. This walk probes farther into this delightful dale, reaching as far as the village of Middlesmoor, where, from its hilltop churchyard, there is a lovely view down the length of the dale into which the final section of the walk is drawn.

🖊 This walk can begin in Lofthouse, and the route is described from there, but it goes up to pass the How Stean car park.

Opposite the post office in Lofthouse, a track runs between cottages to a footbridge spanning the River Nidd. Over the river, cross to the Scar House road and a gate. Go between a barn and a playing field to another gate in a wall corner, after which the Middlesmoor road is encountered. Turn right for a few strides, then bear left onto the road for Stean, soon passing the car park and crossing How Stean Beck. Follow the road as it turns right and passes the entrance to How Stean Gorge.

There is a charge for admission to the How Stean Gorge, a narrow chasm carved through the rocks, and if time allows this should be included in the walk.

Return to the road and turn right, walking as far as a stile at a footpath signposted to Middlesmoor Ⓐ. The ongoing path soon crosses How Stean Beck, and ascends steps to a gate. From the gate, head for a wall gap on the right, and then turn left

Lofthouse village

onto the Nidderdale Way which now leads on across fields to meet the lane into Middlesmoor.

Walk up towards the village, a lovely place perched high above the dale. The church, St Chad's, and its churchyard are well worth visiting. Go past the pub, and just after the final building on the right, turn right onto a track **B**, but turn immediately left through a gate onto a grassy path past a car park.

Cross a stile, and go forward alongside a wall (on the left) to another stile at the western edge of a narrow plantation. Keep on through a gap and tend right in the next field to yet another stile, from which the route maintains much the same direction across more fields and heading for a track that runs to Northside Head Farm.

Turn right along the track and continue beyond the farm, at first still on the track but then alongside a wall on the right to reach a gate at the edge of How Gill Plantation **C**. Here turn right and pass through another gate and start going downhill. Bear left to cross a stream and then aim for a fence/wall corner.

Cross a stile and head for the bottom left-hand corner of a field. Climb stone steps and go ahead to a stile after which head obliquely across the next field to another stile. A short way on the Scar House road is reached **D**.

Cross the road and the field opposite to reach Limley Farm. On reaching the

SCALE 1:25 000 or 2½ INCHES to 1 MILE 4CM to 1KM

farm buildings turn right onto its access track, but soon leave it, on the left, as it turns up towards the valley road. Not long after leaving the farm, once more along a stretch of the Nidderdale Way, the route crosses the line of the River Nidd, which does not always have water in it.

Across the river, pursue a track known as Thrope Lane, which takes a slightly elevated course, with lovely views, to intercept a road that leads directly back to Lofthouse. ●

walk | 5

Start
Grassington

Distance
5 miles (8km)

Height gain
655 feet (200m)

Approximate time
2½ hours

Route terrain
Limestone uplands; woodland tracks; riverside paths; some road walking

P Parking
National Park car park, Grassington (Pay and Display)

OS maps
Landranger 98 (Wensleydale & Upper Wharfedale), Explorer OL2 (Yorkshire Dales – Southern & Western areas)

GPS waypoints

- SE 002 637
- Ⓐ SE 002 644
- Ⓑ SD 998 651
- Ⓒ SD 992 660
- Ⓓ SD 988 655
- Ⓔ SD 982 652
- Ⓕ SD 991 645

Grassington and the River Wharfe

Grassington, capital of Upper Wharfedale, surrounded by limestone moorland, woodland and with riverside paths radiating from it in all directions, is a walker's paradise. Not surprisingly, given the extravagant beauty of these surroundings, the Dales Way wanders through here, and part of it is used to start this walk which later turns into a woodland nature reserve before dropping to the River Wharfe for the final stage back to Grassington.

Leave the car park and turn left and, a short way on, go right up Grassington's main street, which is lined with shops, pubs and cafés.

> **Grassington**
> The cobbled market square is especially attractive, as are many of the old stone houses built from the 17th to the 19th centuries. Three hundred years ago, Grassington was a small farming centre that later expanded as lead mining, textile and quarrying industries developed. Today, Grassington thrives on tourism.

Go up the main street and near the top turn left into Chapel Street. Leave the street at Bank Lane Ⓐ, by turning right onto the Dales Way footpath (signposted to Kettlewell), and soon enter a walled track. Follow this until the track forks (at gates), and here leave it by turning left through a narrow metal gate. Cross the ensuing field to a through-stile in a wall opposite. Over this, bear left, descend a short distance to a signed and gated gap-stile on the right, and after this strike across the next field to a very narrow squeeze- stile. Cross the next pasture, following a broad, grassy path to the far side of the field, where it bears left beside a wall. Pass a wall gap and locate another squeeze-stile a few strides farther on. Go through this, and head for another a short distance away, there entering Lea Green, site of ancient settlements Ⓑ.

Just after passing through the intake wall, the ongoing track forks. Branch left along a broad grassy track, which a short way farther on forks again. This time branch right through Lea Green and onto the edge of a limestone escarpment, heading towards a wall at the eastern boundary of Bastow Wood.

The path continues roughly parallel with the woodland boundary wall and eventually is joined by a grassy vehicle track from the right, immediately after which the route reaches a ladder-stile and gate 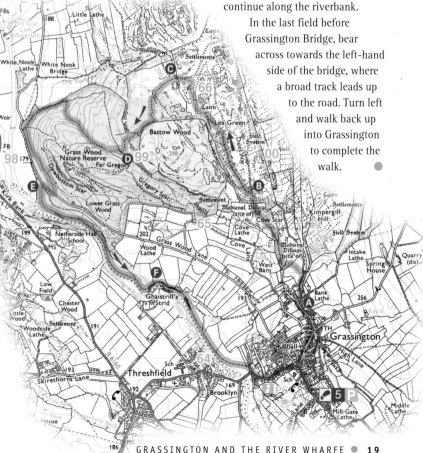**C**. Over this, go into Bastow Wood, initially keeping forward between low hills but gradually swinging round into woodland cover and pressing on to reach a ladder-stile at the edge of the Grass Wood Nature Reserve, managed by Yorkshire Wildlife Trust.

Over the stile, go forward on a clear track that leads down to intercept a broad track at a signpost **D**. Turn right (signposted for Grass Wood Lane), and follow the track, ignoring all branching paths, as it descends through the nature reserve. Eventually, the track leads down to Grass Wood Lane. Just before

reaching the lane, bear left on a woodland path, remaining within the reserve, until you emerge onto the lane. Turn right and walk along the lane for 100 yds, as far as a metal gate **E** on the left. Through this, follow a clear path that descends to the Wharfe. Go left, with the river. After a while, the path climbs above the river, and when it forks take the right-hand branch, descending once more to the riverbank, and continuing forward, following the river to the sweeping S-bend at Ghaistrill's Strid **F**.

Head for a nearby ladder-stile, beyond which a path runs on beside a wall and above the river. Maintain the same direction, crossing four stiles and/or gates to reach a large riverside pasture. Head for a footbridge spanning an in-flowing stream, and then continue along the riverbank.

In the last field before Grassington Bridge, bear across towards the left-hand side of the bridge, where a broad track leads up to the road. Turn left and walk back up into Grassington to complete the walk. ●

SCALE 1:27 777 or 2¼ INCHES to 1 MILE 3.6CM to 1KM

walk 6

Start

Aysgarth (near Yore Bridge)

Distance

5¼ miles (8.5km)

Height gain

690 feet (210m)

Approximate time

2½ hours

Route terrain

Riverside paths; farmland; some road walking

P Parking

Aysgarth Falls car park, just south of church (Pay and Display)

OS maps

Landranger 98 (Wensleydale & Upper Wharfedale), Explorer OL30 (Yorkshire Dales – Northern & Central areas)

GPS waypoints

- SE 011 884
- **Ⓐ** SE 025 888
- **Ⓑ** SE 035 887
- **Ⓒ** SE 017 866
- **Ⓓ** SE 016 868
- **Ⓔ** SE 015 877

West Burton

West Burton lies near the junction of Wensleydale and the tributary valleys of Bishopdale and Walden. This modest walk begins with a stroll alongside the River Ure, then heads up to the remains of a hillside chapel before taking an exhilarating ridge walk to the lovely village of West Burton. It concludes with a little climbing before descending to Palmer Flatts and the parish church.

Leave the car park and turn right, shortly turning into the grounds of St Andrew's Church. Pass to the right of the church and go down an enclosed pathway to a narrow gated gap-stile.

> ### St Andrew's Church
>
> The church of St Andrew, the parish church of Aysgarth, stands on the site of a church built in the 10th century, though most of the existing church is 19th century. It is especially renowned for the Jervaulx Screen in the chancel, regarded as the best screen in Yorkshire. The vicar's desk is also quite elaborate.

Pass through another gate and climb easily to the edge of a small woodland. Once through this bear left along a broad grassy path which shortly brings the Aysgarth Falls into view,

Wensleydale pastures

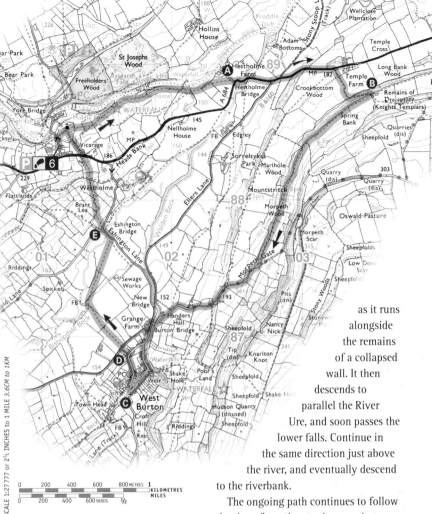

as it runs alongside the remains of a collapsed wall. It then descends to parallel the River Ure, and soon passes the lower falls. Continue in the same direction just above the river, and eventually descend to the riverbank.

The ongoing path continues to follow the river, from time to time passing through gated gap-stiles, and finally bearing diagonally across a field to reach the valley road at Hestholme Bridge **Ⓐ**. Cross the bridge and follow the road, climbing a little, for almost $^1/_2$ mile, *taking care against approaching traffic,* and finally leaving the road at two signposted footpaths on the right, near a farm.

Take the left-hand footpath, signposted for Templars Chapel. The path follows a wall and leads to a gate at the bottom of a wooded slope, and gives onto a rising stony track. At the top of the track **Ⓑ**, the route turns abruptly right onto a footpath signposted for Morpeth Gate. First, take

SCALE 1:27,777 or 2½ INCHES to 1 MILE 3.6CM to 1KM

a moment to go into the adjacent field to visit the remains of the Penhill Preceptory.

The continuing footpath runs at the top edge of woodland, and eventually passes through a gate and goes on to intercept a stony track (Morpeth Gate). Now turn right, heading down the track, which ends at the road leading, left, into West Burton. Go towards the village, and shortly, as the road bends right, keep ahead for the village centre. Walk up the left-hand side of the village green, and then, at the far side (near the telephone box) **C**, circle right to come back down to pass the village shop. Just after passing the shop, bear left, heading out of the village. As the road bends to the right, leave it by turning left onto a narrow and enclosed path at the side of the Reading Room **D**, signposted for Eshington Bridge.

Steps lead down to a road. Go right and immediately left at another footpath sign, and head down-field, aiming to the left of a barn. After the barn, keep to the right of overhead powerlines, heading for a stile in the far corner of the field. Walk to another stile nearby, and from this, bear right, shortly walking alongside a wall to a step-stile. Now cross the middle of a large pasture to reach the road near Eshington Bridge **E**.

Turn left to cross the bridge, and then bear right with the main road, but almost immediately leave it at a footpath signposted for Palmer Flatts. Walk up-field aiming for a powerline pole and another stile just beyond it. From this turn right to another gated gap nearby, and climb into the next field, soon bearing right to a gate. A green path, signposts and gap-stiles show the way across a complex arrangement of enclosed fields.

Eventually the path comes out onto the main valley road. Cross and go ahead along a track opposite that leads directly to St Andrew's Church. Continue to the church doors, and there turn left to return to the car park. ●

The remains of Templars Chapel

Pen-y-ghent from Brackenbottom

walk 7

Sulber Nick

Start
Horton-in-Ribblesdale

Distance
5½ miles (8.75km)

Height gain
720 feet (220m)

Approximate time
3 hours

Route terrain
Limestone uplands, a little road walking

P Parking
Horton-in-Ribblesdale (Pay and Display)

OS maps
Landranger 98 (Wensleydale & Upper Wharfedale), Explorer OL2 (Yorkshire Dales – Southern & Western areas)

GPS waypoints
✏ SD 807 726
Ⓐ SD 790 731
Ⓑ SD 777 735
Ⓒ SD 783 746
Ⓓ SD 787 741

So many walkers visiting Horton-in-Ribblesdale are bound either for Pen-y-ghent, or on to Ingleborough. Only a small number explore the extensive limestone landscapes that flank both sides of the valley and in spring, especially, provide a wealth of flora that is breathtaking. This moderate walk passes through a narrow geological feature, Sulber Nick, before traversing typical limestone uplands.

✏ Leave the car park by walking past the toilets to a bridge spanning the River Ribble, and then turn left along the valley road.

When the road bends to the right, keep forward and walk up to the railway station. Cross the line with care, and go up steps

Horton-in-Ribblesdale One of the joys of Horton is its collection of 17th- and 18th-century greystone houses and cottages. The village is old enough to be mentioned in the *Domesday Book*, and it was here that Henry VI came during the Wars of the Roses (1455-87) to evade his enemies.

opposite to enter pasture. Continue ascending into the pasture and cross to a gate in a wall from which you bear half-right across a sloping field, crossing a farm track on the way. Pass through a gate, and take to a clear path across undulating pasture to a gate beyond which, you enter the Ingleborough National Nature Reserve, which is what this walk now explores. The Reserve is especially renowned for its wildlife and geology, not least magnificent limestone pavements. Ingleborough itself, beyond the scope of this walk *(but see Walks 25 and 27)* is also part of this magnificent landscape heritage, which is of international importance.

Beyond the gate a path climbs past waymarks, at the second of which it forks. Here, branch left and climb to a limestone edge to gain more level ground. Keep going to reach a two-way signpost **A**, to which you will eventually return, but for now keep on in the same direction to reach a gate in a wall. Ahead lies an interesting dry valley known as Sulber Nick – all that remains of an old stream long since diverted underground. In spring you'll find cross-leaved heath here on a bed of

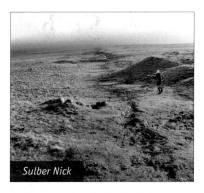

Sulber Nick

dark peat, and probably hart's tongue fern in the grikes of the limestone pavement. Walk up through Sulber Nick until you reach a four-way signpost **B** on the limestone edge. Here turn right (for Selside), now walking along a broad horizontal track. Continue to pass a gate, and when, farther on, the ongoing track forks, branch right following waymarks. The route crosses a large area of limestone pasture with a number of cross tracks to distract you. But keep following the waymarked route and eventually you arrive at a gate giving into a narrow pasture. Bear right to another gate, and on to a vehicle track beside a wall **C**.

Follow the track until it curves right to a wall corner where it branches. Here, bear right, heading for South Houses Farm. Keep on through the farmyard and out along the track beyond, but only as far as a gate on the left (waymarked). Through the gate go down to cross a stream and a through-stile, and then go left across the corner of the ensuing pasture to another stile. Do not cross this, but turn right, re-entering the Nature Reserve **D**, and walk alongside the wall. When the wall changes direction, keep forward on a broad green path that leads back to the signpost passed on the outward route **A**, and from here retrace your outward route, hopefully with a fine view of Pen-y-ghent directly in front of you. ●

SCALE 1:27777 or 2¼ INCHES to 1 MILE 3.6CM to 1KM

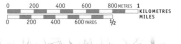

Start

Reeth

Distance

5½ miles (8.7km)

Height gain

540 feet (165m)

Approximate time

3 hours

Route terrain

Riverside paths; farmland; a little road walking

P Parking

Village green, Reeth

OS maps

Landrangers 92 (Barnard Castle & Richmond), and 98 (Wensleydale & Upper Wharfedale), Explorer OL30 (Yorkshire Dales – Northern & Central areas)

GPS waypoints

SE 038 993
Ⓐ SE 035 999
Ⓑ NZ 027 008
Ⓒ NZ 039 002
Ⓓ SE 041 992
Ⓔ SE 046 985
Ⓕ SE 032 989

Reeth, Arkengarthdale and Grinton

Most visitors to this corner of the Dales have arrived from east or west along Swaledale, and it is this beautiful dale that holds many people's attention. But extending northwards from Reeth is the most northerly of the dales, Arkengarthdale, a long and sinuous route into the hills. The first part of this walk investigates Arkengarthdale, while the second heads across riverside meadows to the nearby village of Grinton from where it treks across more riverside fields to a footbridge spanning the Swale and an easy return to Reeth. The contrast between the two halves is distinct and appealing: the one giving a distant view of the wild upper reaches of Arkengarthdale, the other enjoying riparian rambling of the highest order.

Reeth Reeth was formerly an important centre for a lead mining industry, but is today an immensely popular resort for day-trippers who flock here to sample afternoon teas, locally made bread and cakes and the invigorating scenery. The village spreads itself around a green, split by the main road, and has an attractive display of cottages and houses.

From the village green, walk across to the post office and bear left to pass the **Ivy Cottage Tea Room** and then right towards the **Arkleside Hotel**. Just past the hotel, leave the road

Reeth village centre

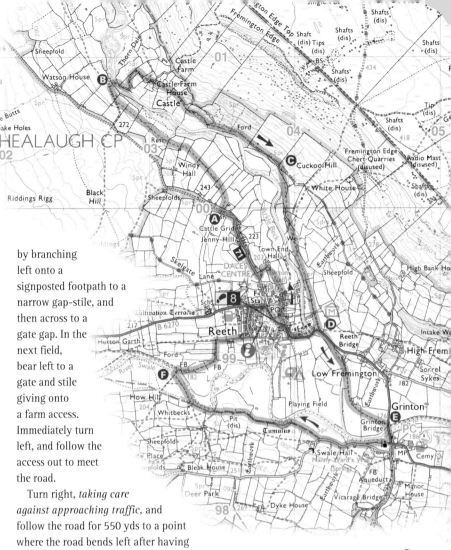

by branching left onto a signposted footpath to a narrow gap-stile, and then across to a gate gap. In the next field, bear left to a gate and stile giving onto a farm access. Immediately turn left, and follow the access out to meet the road.

Turn right, *taking care against approaching traffic*, and follow the road for 550 yds to a point where the road bends left after having crossed a cattle-grid. Here, look for a signposted stile in the wall on the right (for Langthwaite) **A**. In the ensuing field, bear slightly right, but clearly heading up-dale on a grassy path that links a long series of mainly gap-stiles.

Eventually, the ongoing path meets a field vehicle track and descends to a signpost. Here, bear right on the track (signposted for Fremmington (sic)), and go down to cross a bridge **B** spanning the river.

After the bridge, the ongoing track bears right and shortly swings left at a signpost for Fremington. It then climbs gently alongside a wall. A little higher up, the track leaves the wall and bears right, up towards a farm. Ascend to a gate to the right of the farm building, and through this cross to another gated gap-stile. Cross the next field, and then once more follow a clear grassy route across a series of walled pasture, now heading back down the dale.

Continue past a derelict farmhouse and keep on to a signpost beside a pair of old gate pillars. Here, the path forks, with one path descending towards the riverside. Ignore this, and instead keep left onto a gently rising stony track along the base of lightly wooded slope. Keep an eye open for an old limekiln in among the trees.

The path now runs above a wall. Stay on it as far as a metal gate and gap-stile **C**. A barn in the field below bears a large white double arrow. Descend to pass to the right of the barn and down to a gap-stile and cross another field to a second stile. Through this, bear left and once more follow a grassy path across walled pastures linking gap-stiles.

The ongoing path eventually leads on to the edge of Reeth and out to the main road **D**.

Here the walk may be shortened by turning right over a road bridge, soon reaching the village green in Reeth.

For a longer walk, turn left on reaching the road, following it for about 165 yards to a signposted footpath at a kissing-gate for Grinton.

The path passes a farm, and then, as a grassy path, crosses a large riverside pasture, and then across more pastures to steps leading up onto Grinton Bridge **E**. Turn right over the bridge and walk to the village, taking the first gate giving access into the churchyard.

Walk along the lane until it bends left, and there leave it by bearing right onto a signposted bridleway that runs

> ### Grinton
>
> During the Middle Ages, Grinton, which is an older settlement than Reeth, was the only place in the dale with a church. Dedicated to St Andrew, the present church is mainly 15th century, but parts of it date to the 12th century, and it has held a key influence on the life of dales people since that time. It is a low, grey church but of considerable interest with a lovely Jacobean pulpit and a drum-shaped Norman font.

between walls. This walled track leads on to a gate giving into the bottom corner of a sloping pasture. Turn right alongside a fence, and keep forward through a gate, still beside a fence, and continue to reach a gravel track. Turn right on this to a footbridge spanning the Swale **F**. This was damaged by flood water a few years ago and only reinstated in December 2002, at a cost of £113,000; hopefully it will prove more robust than the 1920s original.

Over the bridge turn right to a narrow gate and continue on a grassy track across an enclosed pasture to a low footbridge giving onto a narrow walled track to the right of a barn.

Continue up the track. At the top, turn right for Reeth, though a thoughtfully positioned bench encourages a moment of retrospective viewing. The track shortly becomes a surfaced lane. Continue to the first turning on the left. Go left here (Langhorne Drive) and walk up to the main road and there turn right to return to the village green. ●

Farm cottage, Arkengarthdale

Aysgarth Falls and Bolton Castle

walk 9

A pleasure at any time of year, though especially beautiful in lamb-spring, this delightful circuit from Aysgarth to the village of Castle Bolton and back is easy walking. Lord Scrope's great endeavour, the ancient Bolton Castle, considered to be 'a climax of English military architecture', is an added pleasure.

Start
Aysgarth Falls Visitor Centre

Distance
6 miles (9.9km)

Height gain
575 feet (175m)

Approximate time
3 hours

Route terrain
Mainly farmland; riverside paths; a little road walking

Parking
Visitor centre car park (Pay and Display)

OS maps
Landranger 98 (Wensleydale & Upper Wharfedale), Explorer OL30 (Yorkshire Dales – Northern & Central areas)

GPS waypoints
SE 012 887
Ⓐ SE 030 900
Ⓑ SE 039 910
Ⓒ SE 025 912
Ⓓ SE 011 900

Set off from the National Park visitor centre at Aysgarth and walk out towards the road, following a fenced pathway to the right, shortly crossing the road and going through a gate onto a broad track (signposted to Middle Falls and Lower Falls). The track leads into Freeholder's Wood, which is an ancient woodland where the National Park authority has reintroduced traditional hazel coppicing to regenerate the wood and provide wildlife habitats. Some of the residents of nearby Carperby still have rights of estover in Freeholder's Wood, i.e. the right to take wood, usually for burning, house or hedge repairs, from a forest.

A brief diversion, right, down steps visits the Middle Falls, a splendid sight when the river is in spate; return to the main track and turn right, and press on to the Lower Falls. Another short deviation leads to a viewpoint for these falls. On the return from the falls, at a path junction, turn right and follow the ongoing path above the river to a stile. Over this, walk beside an intermittent hedgerow on the left, to a fence. Here turn right and walk beside the fence to a stile.

Cross the ensuing field in much the same direction, but bearing slightly left on a broad green track towards Hollin House Farm. At the farm, go right on its access lane, and on reaching open pastureland (at a gate) keep forward a short distance to a signpost, and here branch right, through a gate and onto a track beside a fence, heading for a stile in a distant wall.

In the pasture beyond, go forward on a green track with Bolton Castle now in view off to the left. The track leads down to a wall at a signpost (Castle Bolton). Bear right alongside the wall (do not go through the gap-stile in the wall), to a gate and gap-stile in a wall corner. Beyond, continue with the wall on your right, and when it bends right, leave it and go forward onto another green path that moves across to accompany another wall on the right to enter the enclosed Thoresby Lane Ⓐ at a gate and stile.

Follow the lane (seasonally overgrown) to Low Thoresby Farm, where the track becomes surfaced. Go around the farm and walk out to meet the main road on the edge of Redmire, at a T-junction. Turn left, *and taking care against approaching traffic*, follow the road.

About 65 yds after the road bends to the left, leave it, on the right, through a concealed gap-stile **B** (ignore an earlier footpath for Redmire), and then follow an obvious green path across a series of fields linked by stiles. Shortly after a small barn on the right, continue forward, but then keep an eye open for a gated gap-stile in the wall on your left. Through this continue beside the wall, soon to cross the trackbed of the former Wensleydale Railway, before continuing into Castle Bolton. At the village, turn left and walk towards the castle.

> **Bolton Castle** The castle was built in 1379 for Richard de Scrope, Lord Chancellor of England between 1378 and 1380, at the start of Richard II's reign. Lord Scrope (1327-1403), a retainer of John of Gaunt, Duke of Lancaster, raised his family to the peerage by a career of unremitting service on the battlefield and in administration, which included being Warden of the West March in the troubled regions of the Anglo-Scottish border. He was the eldest surviving son of Chief Justice Henry Scrope, and was occasionally denigrated for his lowly origins. Today, his massive fortress is one of the best preserved in the country, and dominates the surrounding countryside it was built to defend.

Go past the church of St Oswald, with the castle on the left, and along a broad track to pass the entrance to a car park. Just by the entrance, pass through a gate across the track, and immediately

bear left (leaving the track) to a gap-stile in a field corner. Cross a small enclosure, and then from a wall corner descend obliquely left across an open pasture on a footpath waymarked with yellow-topped poles.

On the far side of the pasture, locate and go through another narrow gate/stile and descend to cross

SCALE 1:27777 or 2¼ INCHES to 1 MILE 3.6CM to 1KM

Beldon Beck by a footbridge **C**, rising beyond to another stile. Then continue beside a fence across fields to West Bolton Farm. Pass through a gate directly in front of the farm buildings and follow its access track to locate a gated gap-stile on the right. The ongoing path now runs to the north of a small plantation, and passes through a narrow gate before descending to cross a stream. Over the stream bear right to a stile, and then keep on along an obvious

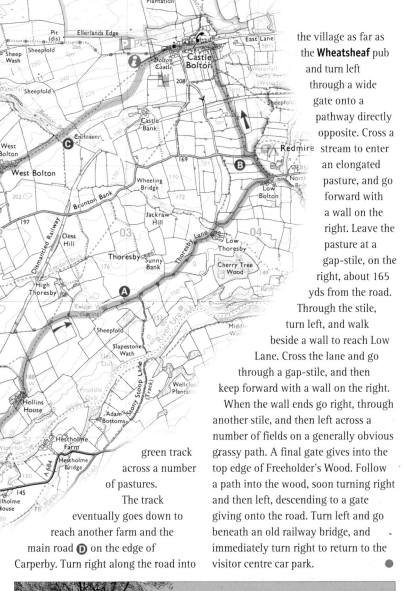

the village as far as the **Wheatsheaf** pub and turn left through a wide gate onto a pathway directly opposite. Cross a stream to enter an elongated pasture, and go forward with a wall on the right. Leave the pasture at a gap-stile, on the right, about 165 yds from the road. Through the stile, turn left, and walk beside a wall to reach Low Lane. Cross the lane and go through a gap-stile, and then keep forward with a wall on the right.

When the wall ends go right, through another stile, and then left across a number of fields on a generally obvious grassy path. A final gate gives into the top edge of Freeholder's Wood. Follow a path into the wood, soon turning right and then left, descending to a gate giving onto the road. Turn left and go beneath an old railway bridge, and immediately turn right to return to the visitor centre car park. ●

green track across a number of pastures.

The track eventually goes down to reach another farm and the main road **D** on the edge of Carperby. Turn right along the road into

Bolton Castle

walk 10

Dentdale

Start
Dent

Distance
6 miles (9.5km)

Height gain
920 feet (280m)

Approximate time
3 hours

Route terrain
Limestone uplands; a little road walking; riverside paths

Parking
Dent (Pay and Display)

OS maps
Landranger 98 (Wensleydale & Upper Wharfedale), Explorer OL2 (Yorkshire Dales – Southern & Western areas)

GPS waypoints
- SD 704 871
- **Ⓐ** SD 698 858
- **Ⓑ** SD 683 864
- **Ⓒ** SD 688 877
- **Ⓓ** SD 693 873
- **Ⓔ** SD 694 879
- **Ⓕ** SD 707 871

Dentdale is noticeably different from the other dales in having most of its fields separated by hedgerows rather than drystone walls, and here the practice of laying hedges still goes on, a wonderfully ecologically friendly way of fencing fields. This walk from the village of Dent begins up a narrow wooded ravine and rises to meet an ancient packhorse trail before sweeping down across hill farmland to meet the River Dee.

Dent The whitewashed cottages, cobbled streets, 12th-century church and splendid location just above the valley river give Dent an inspirational setting. In the 17th and 18th centuries, this was the hub of an extensive hand-knitting industry, but its most famous inhabitant was Adam Sedgwick, Woodwardian Professor of Geology at Cambridge, though one record suggests he was ignorant of matters geological and only began to study the subject on his appointment.

Leave the car park, cross into the lane opposite, and walk up past the village green. Continue in the same direction into the wooded confines of Flinter Gill, through which a stony track rises steadily. This is a former packhorse trail that climbed, as this walk does, to meet the Occupation Road (the 'Ocky) before heading westwards across South Lord's Land into Barbondale. At the top of the ascent a conveniently placed bench offers a moment of retrospective contemplation – and a breather. Go through a gate to meet the Occupation Road at a T-junction **Ⓐ**. Turn right, signposted for Keldishaw.

The 'Occupation Road', an ancient highway dating from 1859, sweeps south across the moorland fellsides and is a delight to amble. Do so for 1¼ miles until the track emerges onto the Barbondale road. There turn right to follow the road for 500 yds, and then leave it at a signposted footpath on the left for Underwood **Ⓑ**.

Follow a broad grassy track that curves around a low hill dotted with limestone outcrops (Stone Rigg) to reach a ladder-stile. Over this, go forward alongside a dilapidated wall, but as this starts to climb the fellside above, the track bears off to the right, and eventually curves around the shoulder of the fell and passes at a distance below the craggy hillside of Combe Scar to reach the ruined Combe House. Go past the derelict farm and continue down a broad track that would once have been its access, to approach the farm at Tofts. Just before Tofts the track

crosses a ford, but this is not the right of way, which lies a little to the left, downstream, crossing the stream by a narrow footbridge. From this climb the bank to reach a metal gate between farm buildings, and through this go forward to a wooden gate, and then follow the farm access past the small group of buildings at Bower Bank and out to meet a narrow lane **C** on the edge of Gawthrop.

Turn right and walk into and through Gawthrop, and on leaving the village also leave the road at a signposted footpath for Barth Bridge **D**. Walk past farm buildings and through a gate, and then continue alongside a fence to a low step-stile giving onto a path above a steep-sided ravine. The subsequent way down-field is well-waymarked and leads to a gated gap-stile on the left. Through this turn immediately right and continue to parallel a wall, which becomes increasingly subdued by an overgrown hedge. This leads to a gate giving onto a road. Turn left to Barth Bridge **E**.

On the bridge, and just before the river, turn right to join the Dales Way (signposted for Hippins), which now leads all the way back to Dent. Set off across a meadow on a green footpath. The route is easy to follow, maintaining company with the river, and for a short stretch emerging onto the road before turning away again (signposted for Church Bridge). At this point, the shortest way back to the start is along the road, *but the riverside alternative is not much longer and provides lovely views of the village and its church.*

Resume the riverside path and follow this until, just after a narrow footbridge, the Dales Way goes up steps at Church Bridge to meet a road. Here **F**, turn right and walk up the road to the village, passing a large, stone memorial to Adam Sedgwick before returning to the car park. ●

SCALE 1:27777 or 2¼ INCHES to 1 MILE 3.6CM to 1KM

Cam Head

Start

Kettlewell

Distance

6 miles (9.6km)

Height gain

1,180 feet (360m)

Approximate time

3½ hours

Route terrain

Farmland; moorland; riverside paths; a little road walking

Parking

Kettlewell (Pay and Display)

OS maps

Landranger 98 (Wensleydale & Upper Wharfedale), Explorer OL30 (Yorkshire Dales – Northern & Central areas)

GPS waypoints

- SD 968 723
- Ⓐ SD 971 725
- Ⓑ SD 970 753
- Ⓒ SD 954 746
- Ⓓ SD 951 744

A steady but fairly easy climb from Kettlewell to Cam Head along a walled green lane is followed by a winding descent along another green lane to the hamlet of Starbotton. The views over Wharfedale are extensive and superb, and the return to Kettlewell is an easy and agreeable walk down the Dales Way, which here uses meadows bordering the River Wharfe.

Kettlewell   Like many villages in the Yorkshire Dales, Kettlewell began as a small farming community, but later expanded as textile and then lead mining industries came into the area. Many of its houses and cottages belong to the heyday of those industries in the 18th and 19th centuries, including the Victorian church.

Begin by turning left out of the car park towards the village centre. Cross the bridge in front of the **Bluebell Hotel** and turn right, following the road to a junction near the post office. Keep ahead at this junction onto the Leyburn road, shortly turning left with it as it climbs a very steep gradient. A short way on, as the road bends to the right, leave it by going forward onto a walled, stony track Ⓐ.

The track is Top Mere Road; it climbs steadily, though the gradient eases higher up, allowing time to take in the surrounding countryside.

Eventually, the enclosing wall ends, but the track maintains the same direction across the open moorland that rises to Cam Head where the people who lived in the valley came to gather peat for their fires. The track, now a wide and rutted affair, pushes on to meet another track, Starbotton Cam Road, at a signpost.

Go left here Ⓑ, initially still climbing, then levelling before heading down to a gate giving into another walled lane. This lane descends steadily, twisting and turning, as it leads down to Starbotton, providing lovely views up and down Wharfedale along the way.

On reaching the edge of Starbotton, turn left, walking through the streets to reach the valley road at the southern edge of the hamlet Ⓒ. Cross the road with care into a signposted and walled path opposite that leads down to a bridge spanning the River Wharfe Ⓓ.

Like Kettlewell, Starbotton is also a legacy of the lead mining era, but is best remembered for its unusual name and the devastation it sustained in 1686 when Cam Gill Beck – that seemingly innocuous stream flowing down to the valley – became swollen during and after a major storm, sending slurry and boulders down the hillside, causing damage to almost all the houses in the hamlet. It was by far the worst flooding ever experienced in the valley.

Now turn left onto the Dales Way which takes the walk back to Kettlewell. The way generally parallels the river, with a few minor deviations, but provides a delightful and easy conclusion to the walk. Just on reaching Kettlewell, the path passes through a gate onto the riverbank and climbs briefly to the western edge of the road bridge, with the end of the walk only a few strides away. ●

Kettlewell from Top Mere Road

SCALE 1:25000 or 2½ INCHES to 1 MILE 4CM to 1KM

Kettlewell and Arncliffe

Start
Kettlewell

Distance
6 miles (9.8km)

Height gain
1,590 feet (485m)

Approximate time
3½ hours

Route terrain
Mainly upland moors; riverside paths; a little road walking

P Parking
Kettlewell (Pay and Display)

OS maps
Landranger 98 (Wensleydale & Upper Wharfedale), Explorer OL30 (Yorkshire Dales – Northern & Central areas)

GPS waypoints
- SD 968 723
- Ⓐ SD 952 722
- Ⓑ SD 933 720
- Ⓒ SD 952 706
- Ⓓ SD 967 703

Two dales are included in this walk, which starts from Kettlewell in Wharfedale and climbs steeply across rugged moorland to drop equally steeply down into Littondale. A delightful stretch alongside the River Skirfare follows before another up-and-over section, rather less demanding than the earlier one, crosses the shoulder of the hills for a stunning view over Wharfedale.

Kettlewell lies on the banks of the Wharfe, surrounded by steep hillsides and moorlands criss-crossed by drystone walls. From the car park the route begins by crossing the Wharfe bridge and immediately turning right, but taking the left-hand one of two tracks, one that rises to a gate and a signpost for Arncliffe. Almost immediately, leave the stony track by branching left onto an ascending path that soon climbs to a through-stile beyond which the path rises more steeply to a limestone scar above.

Pass through the scar by a narrow, rocky gully and continue climbing beyond onto moorland, following a grassy path to a signpost at a cross-track, from which it maintains the same direction, still climbing to reach a ladder-stile over a wall. Over this bear left, parallel with the wall, still climbing but now at an easier gradient. Gradually the route moves away from the wall, bearing right across a limestone plateau but later climbing through a low limestone lip, above which the path heads for another ladder-stile.

After the stile, continue across the top of the ridge to another stile Ⓐ, where the descent to Arncliffe begins as a grassy track across heather moorland. Continue descending to a footpath sign where the track bears right, continuing steadily downwards to a ladder-stile spanning an intake wall at the top edge of mixed woodland. Drop steeply down through the woodland.

The descending path eventually reaches the valley road Ⓑ. Cross to a narrow gate opposite and walk beside the River

Skirfare passing the church. On the far side of the field, go left over the river bridge and walk round to the church.

Here, the route has only touched on the lovely village of Arncliffe, and it is worth taking a short break from the route to explore a little farther.

Go past the lychgate and onto a path beside the churchyard (signposted for Hawkswick), leading through to a riverside pasture. The riverside path is never in doubt, continuing downstream as a mainly grassy track at varying distances from the river, but finally being channelled in towards a footbridge 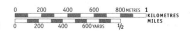 spanning the river and, over it, giving onto a narrow lane beyond. Turn right and walk into Hawkswick.

Leave the village road at a footpath on the left, signposted for Kettlewell, and turn up a stony track between cottages. After a stile the track forks. Branch left and soon curve round above

the intake wall. As it gains height the path moves away from the wall, and continues to climb across the shoulder of Hawkswick Moor. The path climbs steadily to a large cairn **D** and there bears left, still climbing to gain the ridge at a ladder-stile.

Over the stile take the higher of two paths (they soon rejoin), and begin an outstanding high level trek northwards, for the most part descending gently and finally crossing a couple of ladder-stiles to enter a small plantation. Follow the path down and around the edge of the plantation to reach a ruined building. Pass in front of this (i.e. to the right), and continue descending across a lightly wooded slope to emerge onto the valley road. Turn left to return to Kettlewell and the start of the walk. ●

SCALE 1:27777 or 2¼ INCHES to 1 MILE 3.6CM to 1KM

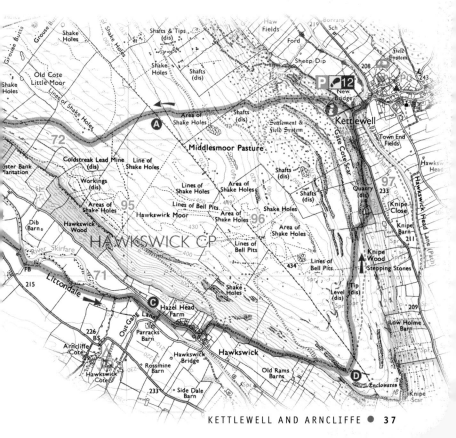

walk 13

Burnsall and Linton

Start
Burnsall

Distance
6½ miles (10.5km)

Height gain
740 feet (225m)

Approximate time
3½ hours

Route terrain
Riverside paths; farmland

Parking
Burnsall (Fee)

OS maps
Landranger 98 (Wensleydale & Upper Wharfedale), Explorer OL2 (Yorkshire Dales – Southern & Western areas)

GPS waypoints
⬛ SE 031 611
Ⓐ SE 025 623
Ⓑ SE 007 630
Ⓒ SE 001 633
Ⓓ SE 003 631
Ⓔ SD 997 625
Ⓕ SE 005 621
Ⓖ SE 025 617

An agreeably relaxing walk through some of Wharfedale's finest scenery, embracing very pleasant riverside walking, an isolated church, two very attractive villages, and, if the river allows, some close encounters with stepping stones.

Burnsall is all that a Dales village should be with its meandering river, arched bridge, a village green, inn, church and Tudor grammar school. The scene is beautiful from every angle.

Leave the village by passing the end of its bridge onto a Dales Way footpath that turns immediately right, near the **Red Lion** pub, to gain the riverbank. A constructed path now leads past the ancient grammar school, founded in 1602, and Burnsall church, which dates from the 14th century.

The path hugs the riverbank all the while, passing shortly through the gorge of Loup Scar. Continue easily to a suspension bridge Ⓐ, by which the river is crossed. The bridge was built by public subscription in the 19th century to replace the stepping stones downriver, though, if the water is very low and your sense of balance good, the stepping stones can still be used – but, please, no heroics here.

On the other side of the bridge, turn immediately left and continue along the true left bank of the Wharfe down an avenue of chestnut, beech and oak trees. Continue following the riverside path, but gradually as the low profile of Linton church comes into view, so the path moves temporarily away from the river, to a gate giving onto a broad track Ⓑ. Just before the gate, another line of stepping stones crosses the river, leading directly to Linton church, but, other than to investigate them, these should be ignored.

Continue along the stony track, which later becomes a surfaced lane. Leave it as it bends right, passing through a gated gap on the left onto a signposted footpath for Grassington and Linton Falls. Now strike across a field, moving back towards the river, across which lies the squat Church of St Michael and All Angels. Keep heading upriver towards a bridge spanning the river at Linton Falls **C**.

> **Linton Falls** This is the fourth bridge to occupy this site; the first, known as Tin Bridge, was built in 1814 and was covered with sheets of metal from old oil drums, hence the name. The present bridge was built in 1989.

Across the bridge turn right along an enclosed walkway that leads to Little Emily's Bridge, an attractive packhorse bridge on the original church path from Threshfield. It is thought to have been named after a member of the Norton family who took refuge nearby at the time of the Civil War.

Turn away from Little Emily's Bridge and go up steps to a road. Turn left, and head for Linton church. If not vistiting the church, just as you reach the last house on the right, about 50 yds past a small parking area (toilets), turn right (signed: B6160 Linton Camp) alongside the gable end **D**.

At the back of the house, the main track bears off to the left, but as it does, leave it through a gap on the right giving onto a path that climbs alongside a wall at a field edge, and eventually runs on to meet a lane. Turn right and walk the lane for a short distance, taking the first turning on the left, towards Linton. As the lane descends into Linton, keep left to reach Linton Beck. Just before the bridge spanning the beck, turn left again, and walk alongside the stream – the village green and **Fountaine Inn** are on the other side. The upper village is dominated by Fountaine Hospital – an almshouse built in 1721 by

SCALE 1:25 000 or 2½ INCHES to 1 MILE 4CM to 1KM

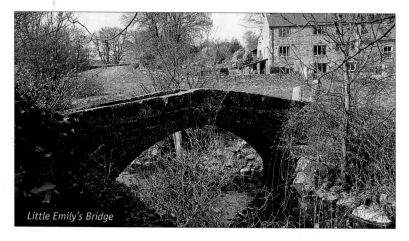
Little Emily's Bridge

Richard Fountaine, a local man who made his fortune as an undertaker in London during the Great Plague. The building was designed by Sir John Vanburgh, and bequeathed to the village as an almshouse, together with an annual sum of £26 to be divided between six poor old men or women from the Linton parish. Linton was formerly the home of Angela Baker, one of the original Calendar Girls (Miss February); following the death of her husband, Angela moved to live in Burnsall.

Without crossing the beck, follow the lane through Linton to Grange Farm, and there **E** turn left onto a footpath for Thorpe Lane. Take a clear, gated route around the farm, and walk out to join a farm track that climbs gently along the edge of hill pasture and then

Thorpe

Thorpe lies concealed among reef knolls, a characteristic that more than likely saved it from the attention of marauding Scots in years gone by. Also known as 'Thorpe-in-the-Hollow', for obvious reasons, the village is a gathering of houses, cottages, a manor house and busy farms. When Fountains Abbey flourished, Thorpe had a reputation for producing shoes and slippers for the monks.

descends to reach a through-stile beside a field gate. From the stile, follow a grassy path across a sloping pasture, aiming for the left-hand edge of a belt of woodland. As you reach the woodland, maintain the same direction, walking across a field to meet Thorpe Lane **F**. Turn left along the lane, a lovely single track road, walled on both sides, as far as a junction, and there turn right towards Thorpe. When the road forks near the village centre, bear left.

Go past the Manor House, after which the lane climbs a little. When it bends to the left, leave it by branching right onto a track (signed for Burnsall). The path sets off between walls and descends through bends to the edge of woodland and a gate. Beyond, the path remains clear and crosses a succession of undulating pastures, pressing on to intercept and cross a rough track (Badger Lane) **G**. Continue much as before, across more undulating fields, but now with Burnsall in view ahead. Gradually, height is lost, and the path runs on as a grassy strip across numerous fields to a narrow path beside a sub-station that gives into the village. At the village lane, turn right and follow it round to the Red Lion pub to complete the walk. ●

Ribblehead &
Chapel-le-Dale

Few can fail to be impressed by the engineering work that between 1869 and 1875 built the Ribblehead viaduct as part of the development of a new route to Scotland from London. It dominates the beginning and end of this walk, though much less so than the bulky fells on either side that culminate to the north in Whernside and to the south in Ingleborough. Most of the walk is flat and easy going, allowing time to contemplate the pastoral surroundings. Some amusement may be found in the abrupt disappearance and re-appearance of streams, a blessing in disguise as crossing them in spate would almost certainly produce wet feet.

Set off along the broad track just to the east of the **Station Inn**, which heads directly for Whernside and the viaduct. As it nears the latter, so it swings left to pass beneath it, and then continues uneventfully towards Gunnerfleet Farm.

Ribblehead Viaduct

The viaduct is a stark reminder of the Midland Railway's determination to construct its own route to Scotland. It was built at enormous cost both in terms of finance and of human life. In the 1980s, affected by the ravages of time and the sheer inhospitability of the climate, the future of the Settle–Carlisle line was called very much into question as the old spectre of financial viability reared its head. During this time a vigorous campaign was waged to keep the line open, and all the effort that went into the campaign was at last vindicated in April 1989, when the Government announced that the line was to remain open. It will long remain as a testament to Victorian endeavour and achievement. From 1989 into the early 1990s, the viaduct saw massive repair work, funded by a consortium comprising British Rail (as it then was), English Heritage, local authorities and other interested bodies, and designed to resolve a problem of water seepage and falling masonry.

After Gunnerfleet Farm, cross Winterscales Beck and turn left along a surfaced field track **Ⓐ**. Shortly after passing through a metal gate, the lane re-crosses Winterscales Beck. Continue as far as another gate beside a cattle-grid **Ⓑ**, and beyond this, leave the lane by branching right onto a grassy track leading to a gate in a wall corner. Keep forward alongside a wall and fence. As the wall bends sharply left, keep ahead, descending

Start
Ribblehead

Distance
6¾ miles (11km)

Height gain
605 feet (185m)

Approximate time
3½ hours

Route terrain
Mainly farmland; a little road walking

P Parking
Near Station Inn, Ribblehead

OS maps
Landranger 98 (Wensleydale & Upper Wharfedale), Explorer OL2 (Yorkshire Dales – Southern & Western areas)

GPS waypoints
  SD 764 791
Ⓐ SD 753 796
Ⓑ SD 747 788
Ⓒ SD 737 771
Ⓓ SD 739 790

towards Winterscales Beck, which, at the crossing point, usually contrives to disappear conveniently underground for a short distance: *in spate conditions, retreat.*

Otherwise, cross to a gate in a corner, and walk on to another a few strides away, and then go forward along the bottom edge of a sloping pasture with a line of larch trees on the right. Bear slightly left to a narrow gate giving into a rocky gully, often flooded (*but by-passable in the adjacent field if the right of way is effectively obstructed*). The gully has limestone as its bedrock, which is slippery when wet. It leads out to join a surfaced lane (Philpin Lane), which is followed out past Philpin Farm to meet the B6255.

Turn right and, *taking care against approaching traffic,* follow the road for 550 yds, as far as the turning on the right to Chapel-le-Dale church. Leave the main road here, and walk up to the church.

Immediately after the church **C**, take the lane on the right, and follow this, ascending steadily to a cattle-grid just beyond which lies Hurtle Pot, a deep hole, its walls swathed in ferns and mosses.

When the ongoing track forks, keep forward (signposted for Ellerbeck) and now on a rough track climbing through an area of mossy boulders and trees. Keep following the track towards Ellerbeck, and, just before the farm, turn right at a shallow ford, and continue up to the farm. There follows an obvious route between the buildings to reach the start of a broad track that takes a gently descending course across sloping pastures.

Keep forward along an obvious track, passing a few farmsteads and eventually reaching a track junction where the route divides with one branch (left) going up beside a barn towards

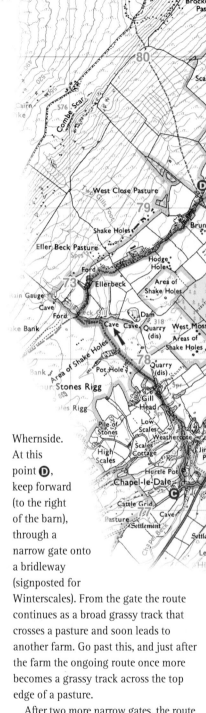

Whernside. At this point **D**, keep forward (to the right of the barn), through a narrow gate onto a bridleway (signposted for Winterscales). From the gate the route continues as a broad grassy track that crosses a pasture and soon leads to another farm. Go past this, and just after the farm the ongoing route once more becomes a grassy track across the top edge of a pasture.

After two more narrow gates, the route passes into a more open area, crossing eventually to a gate and signpost

surfaced lane.

At a track junction near Winterscales Farm, keep ahead over a cattle-grid (signposted to Deepdale), and go past the farm, keeping to the right of the infant Winterscales Beck and soon pass the last of the farm buildings and onto a rising track that curves round to a tunnel beneath the railway at Bleamoor Sidings. Through the tunnel turn right along a constructed path that leads on to rejoin the outward route near the Ribblehead viaduct. ●

SCALE 1:25000 or 2½ INCHES to 1 MILE 4CM to 1KM

beyond at a stream crossing. A short way ahead, the track reaches a house and more farms. At the complex of farm buildings at Ivescar, maintain the same direction, following a

Ribblehead viaduct

walk 15

Burnsall, Trollers Gill and Appletreewick

Start
Burnsall

Distance
7 miles (11.2km)

Height gain
835 feet (255m)

Approximate time
3½ hours

Route terrain
Riverside paths; farmland

Parking
Burnsall (fee)

OS maps
Landrangers 98 (Wensleydale & Upper Wharfedale) and 99 (Northallerton & Ripon), Explorer OL2 (Yorkshire Dales – Southern & Western areas)

GPS waypoints
⌖ SE 031 611
Ⓐ SE 041 607
Ⓑ SE 063 620
Ⓒ SE 067 622
Ⓓ SE 070 623
Ⓔ SE 068 609
Ⓕ SE 047 602
Ⓖ SE 040 606

Two villages, breezy and open moorland, a spectacular ravine and lush riverside meadows combine to make this an agreeably varied walk over countryside that lies between Wharfedale and the more easterly Nidderdale. The ascent, though long, is gradual, and the road walking is along generally quiet roads.

There are two main parking areas in Burnsall: a small car park at the edge of the village, and a large riverside meadow just east of Burnsall Bridge; free parking in the village is limited and usually snapped up early in the day.

Cross Burnsall Bridge and set off along the road for Appletreewick, and, *taking care against approaching traffic*, follow this through the hamlet of Hartlington. Continue to cross the sizeable Barben Beck and on for another 220 yds, leaving the road at a stile and gate Ⓐ on the left giving onto a bridleway for 'New Road'. This starts as a stony track through a shallow ravine, soon emerging to climb beside a wall.

The route, with fine views over Wharfedale, is well signposted and/or shepherded along enclosed tracks, leading first to a group of farm buildings. Here, turn through a gate and keep on along another walled track (still signposted for New Road). When the walls end at a gate, continue to follow the broad track which now crosses upland pasture. Eventually, the track sweeps on across moorland to reach New Road at a gate Ⓑ. Turn left to follow the road, and about 80 yds after the road bends to the right,

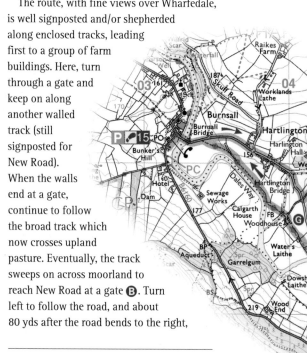

leave it for a signposted footpath on the right (for Skyreholme), following an initially paved section before taking to a waymarked route across rough pasture that descends to intercept a field vehicle track **C**. A short way on the vehicle track sweeps down and to the right following a right of way down to Skyreholme Beck, *an option to be taken after prolonged wet weather, when Trollers Gill can be very slippery.* However, a permissive path (waymarked) branches left from this, just where the track turns to the right. Take to the permissive path, climbing briefly and then shortly descending steeply to a ladder-stile and footbridge spanning Skyreholme Beck. Over the bridge, bear right to another ladder-stile **D**, beyond which you enter the rocky (*and often slippery*) confines of Trollers Gill.

At the bottom of the gill cross a step-stile and keep forward to another giving on to a terraced path above Skyreholme Beck. Pass a large grass-covered mound that once formed the dam of a reservoir that served the

> **Trollers Gill** Trollers Gill is a miniature gorge through the Great Scar limestone, narrow, dark and steep-sided and the classic lair of monsters; indeed, one such resides here, the Barguest, the spectral hound of Craven, a huge, shaggy beast, with yellow eyes as big as saucers. An encounter with the Barguest means almost certain death, few have escaped to tell of it, though there are a number of records of close encounters with the beast.

Skyreholme paper mills. Eventually, the descending track meets a road near the entrance to Parcevall Hall and Grounds **E**. The hall was built in 1671, but has

SCALE 1:25000 or 2½ INCHES to 1 MILE 4CM to 1KM

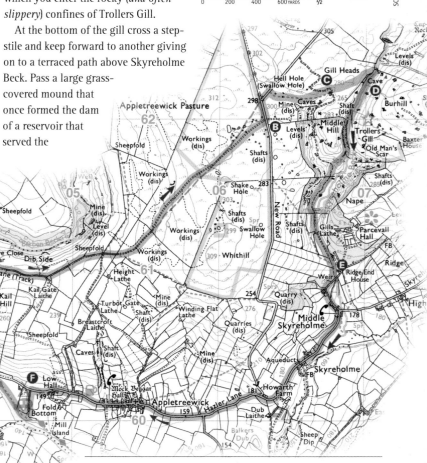

Inside Trollers Gill

an Elizabethan look about it. It is generally regarded as the finest residential building in Wharfedale; the surrounding gardens and **tearoom** are open to the public from Easter until the end of October.

Turn right along the road and continue down to a road junction, there turning right, passing a telephone box, and beginning a long stretch of road walking (*take care against traffic*). The road rolls on through Skyreholme and eventually reaches a road junction. Turn left and continue to Appletreewick.

Press on down through the village, finally leaving the road at the edge of a caravan site by turning left onto a walled footpath **F** for the riverside. On reaching the river, turn right, now following the Dales Way riverside path.

The path leads on to pass Woodhouse Farm **G**, a 17th-century manor house, and once the home of the almost forgotten Wharfedale poet, John Atkinson Bland. Beyond the farm, a footbridge takes the route over Barben Beck once more. From the beck, continue across another field to a gate, after which the path runs on above the Wharfe and finally crosses a large field, used as a car park during summer months, to reach the road. Turn left to recross Burnsall Bridge and return to the start of the walk.

Appletreewick

Appletreewick has more than its share of claims to fame. Of Norse origin, it is recorded in the Domesday Book as in the ownership of the English thanes (low-ranking nobles), Dolfin and Orme. This is a one street village, but few better than this. Fine old buildings line the street from High Hall to Low Hall, and passing by far the best, Mock Beggar Hall, which housed the monks in charge of Bolton Priory's lands hereabouts. But the village is also renowned for a real-life Dick Whittington character, William Craven, born here in 1548. He was sent to London to be apprentice to a merchant tailor and grew in stature and standing to become Sheriff and later Lord Mayor of London.

Clapham, Crummack Dale and Austwick

walk 16

Start
Clapham

Distance
6¾ miles (11km)

Height gain
785 feet (240m)

Approximate time
3½ hours

Route terrain
Farmland; limestone moorland; road walking

Parking
Clapham (Pay and Display)

OS maps
Landranger 98 (Wensleydale & Upper Wharfedale), Explorer OL2 (Yorkshire Dales – Southern & Western areas)

GPS waypoints
SD 745 692
Ⓐ SD 760 691
Ⓑ SD 766 697
Ⓒ SD 771 706
Ⓓ SD 779 692
Ⓔ SD 776 684
Ⓕ SD 765 683

From the attractive village of Clapham, the walk begins by following one of the many walled lanes in this area before making a detour to visit the geological phenomenon known as the Norber Erratics. With superb views all round, the route continues into the remote Crummack Dale, a sweet, green retreat, nothing like so well-visited as other dales, before heading along more walled lanes to the village of Austwick and returning across fields to Clapham. The walk traverses some of the fine limestone scenery.

> **Clapham** Clapham is a village of especial delight, captivating and blessed with old bridges and waterfalls, white cottages, old stone houses and stands of ancient trees. Of its church, the earliest known mention is to what would have been a simple wooden structure, in 1160, when the vicar, Adam, was witness to a legal document. In 1318, following the Battle of Bannockburn, when much of the north of England was defenceless, raiding Scots burned down the church. In the Middle Ages, the replacement church was dedicated to St Michael, although the present structure, substantially rebuilt during the reign of George IV, is dedicated to St James the Apostle.

Leave the car park in Clapham, turn right up Gildersbank and go past the entrance to Ingleborough Hall Outdoor Education Centre.

At the church, bear right and immediately left on a bridleway (signposted for Austwick). The route soon passes through the tunnels of the Ingleborough Estate, and then continues, climbing gently as a stony, walled track.

When the track divides, branch right onto an ancient pack-horse route (Thwaite Lane) that linked Richmond and Lancaster. Follow this for more than ½ mile, and then leave the walled track by branching left at a signpost Ⓐ, and striking across fields for Norber. Head for a wall corner, and then follow the wall to a stile, then continuing directly below Robin Proctor's Scar, and finally climbing a little to reach a signpost Ⓑ.

From the signpost, follow the direction for Crummack, which pursues a narrow path through boulders. Keep the wall on your right in sight and, shortly you will spot a through-stile. Cross this and then walk forward to another similar stile just below a limestone edge (Nappa Scars). After the stile, go forward on a path at the base of the small cliff formed by the scar, after which a clear path continues eastwards, with a wall on your left, to meet a surfaced lane (Crummack Lane).

Turn left along Crummack Lane. The surfacing, however, ends as soon as it reaches Sowerthwaite Farm, and a walled track continues to a junction with another lane on the right **C**. Turn right here, and continue along a winding lane into the hamlet of Wharfe. On reaching Wharfe, at a minor T-junction, turn left, and then almost immediately branch right to continue to follow a walled lane, now heading southwards, to another surfaced lane. Turn right for 150 yds and then at a signposted bridleway **D**, leave the road by branching left towards Wood End Farm, now following Wood Lane.

Just before the farm, bear right along another walled lane and follow this to a track junction **E**. Here take the middle one of three options, remaining on Wood Lane, and follow this out to a road on the edge of Austwick. Turn

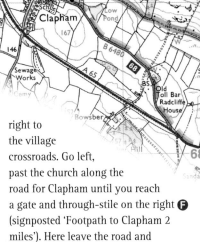

Ingleborough Hall The Hall was formerly the home of Reginald Farrer (1880–1920), a renowned botanist who made repeated journeys to far corners of the world in pursuit of his passion, and brought many foreign plant specimens to Clapham to decorate the grounds of his home.

right to the village crossroads. Go left, past the church along the road for Clapham until you reach a gate and through-stile on the right **F** (signposted 'Footpath to Clapham 2 miles'). Here leave the road and continue up the ensuing field, following an obvious broad green track into a hummocky pasture, and cross to a ladder-stile and gap-stile. Cross the next field to a gated gap. Maintain the same direction in all the following fields, the way now taking an obvious and direct route, linked by gates of one kind or

The way out of Clapham

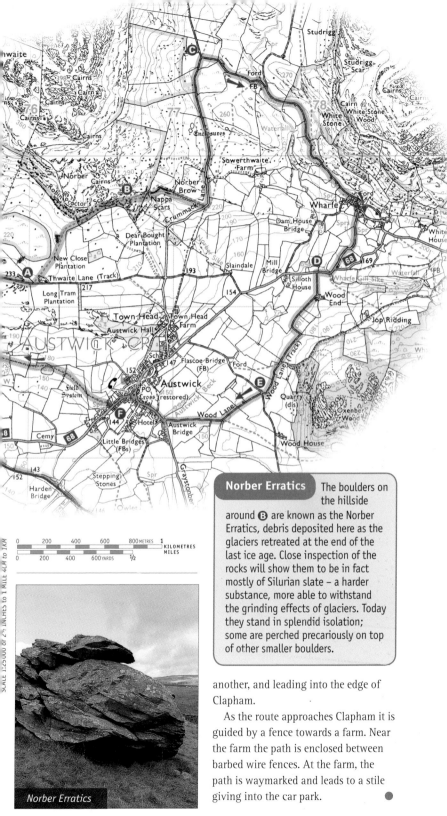

Norber Erratics The boulders on the hillside around **B** are known as the Norber Erratics, debris deposited here as the glaciers retreated at the end of the last ice age. Close inspection of the rocks will show them to be in fact mostly of Silurian slate – a harder substance, more able to withstand the grinding effects of glaciers. Today they stand in splendid isolation; some are perched precariously on top of other smaller boulders.

another, and leading into the edge of Clapham.

As the route approaches Clapham it is guided by a fence towards a farm. Near the farm the path is enclosed between barbed wire fences. At the farm, the path is waymarked and leads to a stile giving into the car park. ●

Norber Erratics

Around Malham

Extend to 9 miles.

walk round Tarn (right side) . by field centre (top) over to watershouses . back down

An easy walk through spectacular limestone scenery. A little *road* scrambling is called for in Gordale, made intimidating by the *its* cascading falls, but not as difficult as it looks. Above the falls a wide limestone plateau opens up to Malham Tarn, followed by a delightful amble back to the top of Malham Cove – but the true splendour of this walk derives from its wealth of geological and botanical interest.

rejoin path at Watsenks

	Start
	Malham

	Distance
	7 miles (11.5km)

	Height gain
	920 feet (280m)

	Approximate time
	3½ hours

	Route terrain
	Farmland; limestone gorges and pavement

	Parking
	Malham (Pay and Display)

	OS maps
	Landranger 98 (Wensleydale & Upper Wharfedale), Explorer OL2 (Yorkshire Dales – Southern & Western areas)

	GPS waypoints
	SD 900 627
A	SD 911 633
B	SD 898 664
C	SD 893 658
D	SD 896 637

> **Malham** The origins of Malham go back to AD700, to a simple settlement centred on the present village green. Around AD1100, the village was cut in two when the beck became the boundary of lands owned by Fountains Abbey and Bolton Priory. Henry VIII's Dissolution of the Monasteries, however, brought new prosperity, replacing old wooden houses by stone buildings that still form the core of the village today. Also surviving to present times is the humped packhorse bridge, built across the beck in 1636.

Leave the car park and follow the road for a short distance towards the village centre. Keep an eye open for a small footbridge across the beck on the right, and use it to gain and follow downstream a broad path on the opposite side (signposted 'Janet's Foss'). A gate gives access to a meadow, the path keeping to its edge, beside the stream. Shortly, pass through a gate not far from an old stone barn, and here change direction. The onward route passing the barn is never in doubt, and leads to a small woodland flanking Gordale Beck, in spring permeated by the strong and garlicky smell of wild ramsons which flower from April to June and especially like damp woodlands.

The head of this shallow gorge is taken by a waterfall, Janet's Foss **A**.

Near the falls a narrow gully leads to a path and a metalled road. Turn right along the road and follow it for a short distance, the towering cliffs of Gordale Scar now in evidence ahead. At a gate on the left, enter beckside pastureland (often used as a camp site) and you can take a path into the very jaws of the chasm. Arguments still rumble quietly as to how this unique rock architecture came into being, some propounding the view that it once formed an enormous cavern which in later times collapsed, leaving only its walls standing, but there is little real doubt

> ### Janet's Foss
> Here, white water tumbles over a lip of tufa into a crystal plunge pool. Tufa is similar to stalagmite in that it, too, is calcium carbonate precipitated from lime-saturated water. Unlike stalagmite, tufa is formed in a surface stream where algae grow and cause the precipitation by altering the chemistry of the water. Along Gordale Beck there are many spots where you will find tufa, some inactive, but some, as at Janet's Foss, still forming. It is most evident at the Foss in the way it projects over a rock ledge to create the cave behind the falls where a legendary fairy queen, Janet, once lived.

that it was cut by retreating meltwater flowing from ice age glaciers.

The path into the gorge gives no indication of what awaits around a sharp corner, for here the walls close in dramatically, 165ft (50m) high and barely 50ft (15m) separating them at one point, severely overhanging at their base, and vertical at their easiest angle. Higher still, more crags and scars continue upwards to the plateau surface above the beck. Hidden from external view, a fine waterfall gushes through an eyehole in a thin wall of limestone, pauses in its downward flight in a natural amphitheatre, and spills splendidly to the broad base of the chasm floor. Close by the eyehole falls, which are actively depositing tufa on a bank below, a larger bank of inactive tufa, to the left, marks the site of an earlier waterfall. This

was active until 250–300 years ago when the beck suddenly discovered its new route through the eyehole.

Many walkers elect to retreat from this point to find an alternative route to Malham Tarn (*see final paragraph*), but by splashing through the shallows it is easy enough (in all but spate conditions) to reach the base of a prominent buttress of banded and inactive tufa dividing the falls, which, improbable though it may seem, offers an entertaining scramble to the sanctuary of the upper gorge. You will get wet, so a small towel and spare socks will help. As with most seemingly difficult things, the start of the scramble poses the problem, but once actually on the rock, the way up is easy – something I've done variously with my father (in his 70s), mother-in-law (in her 60s), young children, and two dogs. *If you do not feel confident about it, then opt for the variant route.*

A good path climbs easily away from the gorge which, from above, can clearly be recognised as a meltwater channel with rocky walls, and across a wide plateau of limestone, the limestone pavement for which this region is so renowned. The path, absorbed now by a rich green fescue turf, broadens and presses on to reach another metalled road (*it would lead, left, back to*

Janet's Foss, Malham

Limestone pavement The
range
of plant life is immense, and quite
remarkable. The fissures between the
blocks (clints) of limestone are called
grykes, and in them, protected from
sun and the attentions of sheep, a
rich variety of woodland and cliff-face
species of plant exists. Hart's Tongue
Fern is but one of a dozen ferns
growing side by side with herb robert,
wood sorrel, dog's mercury and, in a
few secluded spots, baneberry. The
turfed areas, too, have a wealth of
flora: violets, fairy flax, bedstraws
and birdsfoot-trefoil

Malham should the need arise).

Follow the road, right, for a short
distance and continue to a minor
crossroad. Just before the junction the
route crosses the North Craven Fault,
which marks the end of limestone
pavements, for the rock ahead,
supporting Malham Tarn, is
impermeable slate. Keep ahead, and
follow a graded track towards Lings
Plantation **B**, where a left turn, leaving
the main track, shortly leads to the out-
flow of the tarn, a natural lake.

By following the line of the stream
issuing from Malham Tarn the route
regains the road. Turn right to cross the
stream and reach a gate and a path on
the opposite bank **C**.

The water from Malham Tarn
disappears sullenly into stream bed
debris, and from this spot, follow a path
into a deepening dry valley, though the
limestone underfoot can be slippery,
until it curves sharply to avoid a dry
waterfall, Comb Scar. Here the path
doubles about to gain a stile at the head
of a tributary gully which gives easy
access to the floor of Watlowes, which
about 14,000 years ago carried a
powerful meltwater river. In those
distant times the limestone was still
frozen, of course, and prevented the
water sinking underground as it does
today.

Ahead now lies the lip of Malham
Cove, and this unsuspecting approach
is infinitely more dramatic and awe-
inspiring than the easy walk from the
village. No one can fail to be impressed
by the landscape, which is nothing
short of spectacular, and justifies its
popularity on that score. The last few
strides to the lip of the cove are over
slippery limestone pavement, with only
distant views to suggest there might be
an abrupt drop ahead. Walkers with a
good head for heights can approach the
very edge for an aerial perspective of
the people below: *anyone else should*

Malham Tarn A small dam, built in 1791, stabilises the level of the lake, the
overflow of which, Malham Water, flows south under the road
and across the North Craven Fault where it encounters limestone and promptly
disappears underground at a spot labelled, unimaginatively, Water Sinks.

The scenery around Malham and its tarn has been the inspiration of many,
including John Ruskin, and Charles Kingsley, who wrote part of *The Water-Babies*
while at Malham Tarn House as a guest of millionaire Walter Morrison. Charles
Darwin, too, found the unrivalled setting conducive to his studies.

Logic suggests that the waters from Malham Tarn are those which emerge in due
course at the foot of Malham Cove, but this is not so. Tests were first carried out in
the 1870s, and again 100 years later, which demonstrate that the waters of Malham
Tarn issue at Aire Head Springs, to the south of Malham village. For this reason
Malham became famous as one of the places where it was shown that underground
streams are capable of crossing over one another independently in a complex
system of limestone hydrology.

The Dry Valley, Malham

stay well clear.

Across to the right, the limestone pavement may easily be followed to a gate at the top of a staircase. Only a few minutes are needed to descend to the valley floor, where a left turn will lead to the base of the cliff. In the centre, where a small dry valley cuts in, the height of the wall is 230ft (70m). The span of the cove is about 655ft (200m), with grassy ledges reaching in from the edges, but never quite meeting in the middle. Malham Beck, the infant River Aire, here issues from a small pool at the foot of the cliff, and despite cave-diving efforts, limited by a low underground passage, the caves behind the cove remain a mystery.

After leaving the cliffs of Malham Cove, watch for a clapper bridge on the left **Ⓓ** crossing the stream to a gate. From the gate climb diagonally right to a small plateau of fescue turf and continue ascending gently to a prominent stile beyond which a good path works its way back to Malham by a succession of narrow walled lanes, reaching the village close by the humped packhorse bridge and the village green.

Leaving the cove is like passing through an open museum of farming history. The drystone walls across the valley date from the Enclosure Acts, about 200 years ago. Above the beck may be observed a series of horizontal ledges, linchets, or lynchets, built almost 1,000 years ago to improve the land, while low grass ridges across the valley floor, better picked out in late evening sunlight from above the cove, are now all that remain of Celtic field boundaries from about 2,000 years ago.

Walkers not wishing to tackle the ascent of Gordale Scar, should simply retreat to the road and walk back towards Janet's Foss, but only as far as a bridge on the right. Here, go through a gate onto a path signposted for Malham Cove. Cross the ensuing field to a wall corner and then bear right, uphill, beside a wall. Cross a ladder-stile and another field to go up steps to a gate. Bear left along a clear path beside a wall. Beyond another gate, the path continues climbing steadily, curving right to a kissing-gate giving onto a lane. Turn right and follow the lane, and in due course, rejoin the original line. ●

Buckden and Langstrothdale Chase

walk 18

Start
Buckden

Distance
7 miles (11.2km)

Height gain
920 feet (280m)

Approximate time
3½ hours

Route terrain
Mainly upland moors; riverside paths; a little road walking

Parking
Buckden (Pay and Display)

OS maps
Landranger 98 (Wensleydale & Upper Wharfedale), Explorer OL30 (Yorkshire Dales – Northern & Central areas)

GPS waypoints
SD 942 774
Ⓐ SD 944 790
Ⓑ SD 921 789
Ⓒ SD 905 790
Ⓓ SD 932 779

This walk climbs to the tiny hamlet of Cray from Buckden, before heading across the southern slopes of Yockenthwaite Moor to Scar House, where the Quaker tradition flourished strongly in the 17th and 18th centuries. From there the high level traverse continues until the route drops to Yockenthwaite to begin a return leg along a delightful riverside section of the Dales Way.

Buckden, which means the 'valley of the bucks', has been the abode of deer since medieval times, part of an ancient hunting forest. It is a beautiful place, hemmed in on all sides by rounded fellsides and wild moorland.

Go through a gate at the northern end of the car park, and head up a wide track that ascends easily through Rakes Wood. At first the track rises through trees and rocks, but higher up becomes more open; as a gate is approached so the angle of ascent eases, and soon a track deviates uphill towards higher ground. Ignore this, it leads up to Buckden Pike. Instead, continue ahead along the level edge of a limestone escarpment.

At a wall and gate with a narrow stile to the right, squeeze through the stile and keep forward for a short distance to a narrow gate Ⓐ on the left, near a footpath sign. The elevation gained thus far provides a splendid view of the limestone scenery of Upper Wharfedale and Langstrothdale.

Striding out above Cray

Scar House

Scar House is a place where the new religion of the Quakers flourished. The Society of Friends, as it became known, was largely inspired by George Fox, whose vision on Pendle Hill of 'a great people in white raiment by a riverside, coming to the Lord' sent him preaching across the northern parts of England. George Fox is known to have visited Scar House twice, in 1652 and 1677, though it is unlikely the remains of Scar House that appear today are of the actual house he knew.

From the gate the descent to Cray is steep at first and leads down beside a wall to a footpath sign, and on to a gate. Cray Gill is crossed by a shallow ford or nearby stepping stones, to meet the road. Continue behind the **White Lion** pub onto a broad farm track for Yockenthwaite. Pass farm buildings to a gate giving onto a broad track. A short way farther on, when the track forks at a signpost, keep right, to a gate. From the gate the continuation is clear enough, and follows the edge of the escarpment, with only one slight deviation to cross Crook Gill by a footbridge. Keep ahead along a level grassy ledge.

The ongoing path stays above the intake wall, continuing to a signpost **B** above and just beyond Scar House.

The ongoing route continues easily enough above Langstrothdale, a hunting forest that was the preserve of the earls of Northumberland. The valley was originally settled by Norse farmers, and their legacy remains in the place

Crossing stepping stones, Cray

names – Hubberholme and Yockenthwaite – which are still in use.

From the signpost, stay above the intake wall, head for another signpost nearby indicating the way through a gate and stile for Yockenthwaite. A delightful path now skims along the limestone edge below Yockenthwaite Moor, crossing a succession of gated pastures and passing briefly through woodland before starting the descent to Yockenthwaite. On reaching a broad stony track, bear left downhill to the farm at Yockenthwaite **C**, where the Dales Way is encountered.

Go past a signpost and join an access track from the nearby Yockenthwaite Bridge. Head for and pass through gates, and then bear right through a gated gap, beyond which you descend to a riverside path, which, with little deviation from the river, leads to Hubberholme.

At Hubberholme, pass round the church and over the Wharfe Bridge to

Hubberholme

Hubberholme is a delightful spot. Its pub, the **George Inn**, is a long-standing venue for an annual land-letting ceremony held on the first Monday in each year, and which takes the form of an auction by candlelight at which bids are made for the use of a pasture owned by the church. The church itself is interesting, having been built as a forest chapel, and in 1241 given to the monks of Coverham Abbey.

turn left along the road, heading back towards Buckden. Before long, leave the road for a path on the left **D** which loops alongside the Wharfe, a safer option than walking down the road, which is very busy in summer. Eventually, the path does rejoin the road not far from Buckden Bridge, beyond which the village is only a short uphill stroll away. ●

walk 19

Pen-y-ghent

Start
Horton-in-Ribblesdale

Distance
6 miles (9.5km)

Height gain
1,610 feet (490m)

Approximate time
3½ hours

Route terrain
Good tracks and upland paths, mainly across limestone

Parking
Horton-in-Ribblesdale
(Pay and Display)

OS maps
Landranger 98 (Wensleydale & Upper Wharfedale), Explorer OL2 (Yorkshire Dales – Southern & Western areas)

GPS waypoints
SD 807 726
Ⓐ SD 823 743
Ⓑ SD 836 727
Ⓒ SD 816 722

Like an ancient galleon, Pen-y-ghent's two-tiered prow sails purposefully across the surrounding countryside, drawing thousands to its summit each year. The hill is the lowest of the Yorkshire 'Three Peaks', but makes up for it by being the only one to entertain the Pennine Way. It lies barely two miles (3.2km) by crow from the valley of the Ribble which it overlooks, and its ascent need occupy little more than half a day.

Pen-y-ghent Opinions differ as to the meaning and origin of the name, Pen-y-ghent, which despite a once strong Norman influence in the valley below, must derive from the Celtic, from the Kingdom of Brigantia and the tribes forced into what were then remote regions by Roman and Teutonic settlers. Generally thought to mean 'Hill of the Winds', but believed by others to mean 'Hill of the Border Country', its name unquestionably comes from the Welsh language, rendered *Pen y Gwynt* and *Pen y Cant* respectively, – cant meaning a rim.

The walk begins in the straggling village of Horton-in-Ribblesdale, mentioned as a farming community in the *Domesday Book* (1086–87), and to which King Henry VI came during the Wars of the Roses (1455–85) to hide from his enemies.

From the car park turn right to a track on the left leaving the road just past the **Pen-y-ghent Café**, and follow the signposted Pennine Way, which despite heading north east is, in fact, the southbound route. A steady amble of over 1½ miles along the walled path leads easily to the fell-gate, with Pen-y-ghent looming large to the right. This route, Horton Scar Lane, is part of an ancient packhorse road once used to cross to Littondale.

Horton Scar Lane is easy walking, gaining height almost imperceptibly.

On the right, a dry valley is a reminder of the underground drainage system which permeates these hills. Above all this, at the fell-gate **(A)** the route turns sharply right, but another prominent track continues ahead to Hull Pot, a great square-cut hole which looks almost as if it is man-made. The pot is only 330 yds beyond the gate, so it is worth a few minutes to make the diversion.

By way of contrast, return to the fell-gate and pursue the path which leads steadily upwards to the rim of Pen-y-ghent, a direct and conspicuous route to the edge of the escarpment, where it turns abruptly right, and eases along the edge before a final short scamper to the summit. The view is now quite expansive, typical of the fine airy panoramas for which the Pennines are justly famous.

Hull Pot In dry weather no water enters the pot, but when it is wet, with upstream sinks constricted, the resulting waterfall in Hull Pot is a splendid sight. Despite its massive size, there are times, perhaps once or so each year, when the pot fills up completely. Normally all the water sinks beneath the boulders, but this route, too, is constricted so that in times of full flood the water overflows down the dry valley.

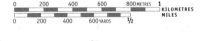

SCALE 1:25000 or 2½ INCHES to 1 MILE 4CM to 1KM

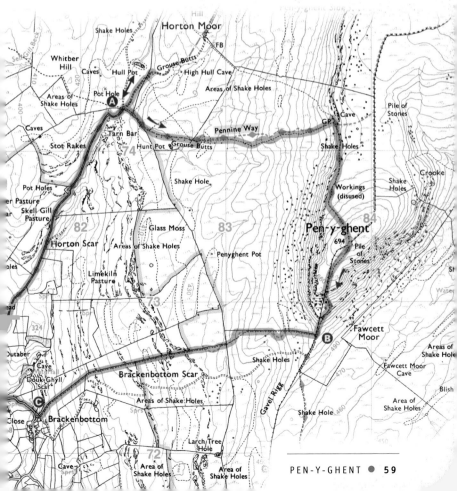

Hull Pot

A wall crosses the summit of Pen-y-ghent, and just over it a triangulation pillar and a large cairn mark the highest ground. Immediately in front of them the path heads right to the prominent tiered southern end of the mountain, where the easy path abruptly ends. A rocky descent now follows, in the first of two stages. Neither is especially difficult, except perhaps in winter conditions, but hands, feet and bottoms are often employed here.

The second rock step has a narrow path running along the edge, and this despite its proximity to the rolling hill-side has a more secure feel about it than nearby rocks, which are quite slippery when wet. In a matter of minutes, below all the rockwork, a couple of stiles are encountered on the right **B**. Here, leave the Pennine Way, cross the stiles and begin the long but easy and enjoyable descent to Brackenbottom **C**.

Turn right on reaching the minor road at Brackenbottom, and follow this out to arrive in a short while on the main valley road, near St Oswald's Church. The church dates from the early 11th century, but has seen restoration work in 1400, when the tower was added, 1823 and 1879, as well as in modern times.

To the right the car park is now only a few minutes away along the road. ●

The Nine Standards

walk 20

Sedbergh and Winder

Start
Sedbergh

Distance
7 miles (11.5km)

Height gain
1,445 feet (440m)

Approximate time
4 hours

Route terrain
Upland moors; riverside paths; farmland; some road walking

Parking
Sedbergh (Pay and Display)

OS maps
Landranger 97 (Kendal & Morecambe), Explorer OL19 (Howgill Fells & Upper Eden Valley)

GPS waypoints
SD 658 920
Ⓐ SD 652 923
Ⓑ SD 658 937
Ⓒ SD 641 929
Ⓓ SD 637 919
Ⓔ SD 637 912
Ⓕ SD 647 910

Creating a bridge between the Pennines and the fells of Cumbria are the Howgills, which rise immediately to the north of Sedbergh. Their smooth, grassy, rounded slopes provide both excellent walking and dramatic scenery. This walk tackles one of the lower fells, Winder (pronounced to rhyme with 'bin'), which is easily if a little energetically accessible from Sedbergh. The route completes its circular tour by strolling along the banks of the River Rawthey using part of the Dales Way.

Sedbergh

From almost any point in the narrow streets of Sedbergh, the Howgills can be seen, their steep slopes presenting a dramatic backcloth to the town. Sedbergh is a small, stone-built town, and became part of Cumbria only in 1974, even though it remains in the Yorkshire Dales National Park, and clearly has many 'Dales' affinities. The town was formerly in the West Riding of Yorkshire, and is largely one long main street. It is an ancient market town with a charter dating from 1251, and is mentioned in the Domesday Book as among the many manors held by Earl Tostig of Northumbria. Today the fame of the town rests on the laurels of its school, set in parkland on the edge of the town. It was founded in 1525, and has grown steadily to earn a national reputation.

In spite of its administrative connections with Cumbria, Sedbergh remains one of the largest towns in the Yorkshire Dales National Park, and is the main western gateway to the Dales. The Turnpike Acts of 1761 brought improvements to the Askrigg–Kendal and Lancaster–Kirkby Stephen roads, both of which pass through Sedbergh, and these improvements made the town more accessible as a staging post for commercial routes across the Pennines. There followed a time of industrial growth as the domestic knitting trade was augmented by a cotton industry based on mills at Birks, Howgill and Millthrop.

The walk begins from the Loftus Hill car park near the church. Leave the car park and turn right, walking up to a T-junction near the Old Reading Room, now the public library. Turn left and then take the first on the right after the post office. The road rises gently and then continues, shortly going round a children's play area. Keep on towards a small housing estate on the upper edge of Sedbergh. Just past the houses, leave the road by turning right onto a narrow, hedgerowed lane (signposted Permissive Path to the fell) Ⓐ that leads up to Lockbank Farm.

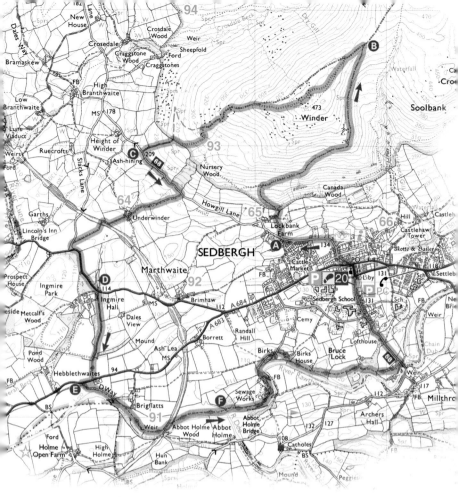

SCALE 1:27777 or 2¼ INCHES to 1 MILE 3.6CM to 1KM

0	200	400	600	800 METRES	1

KILOMETRES
MILES

0	200	400	600 YARDS	½

Go forward through a metal gate (waymarked) and up a broad walled track to a fell-gate. Through this turn left, climbing beside a wall. Almost immediately, leave the wallside path by ascending on the right, along a clear path crossing the hillside, climbing steeply. This shortly bears right and rises through bracken, in due course closing in on a small stream where it intercepts a broader, grassy track.

Turn right towards a shallow col ahead, beyond which the path continues rising at an easier angle across the southern slopes of Winder. Eventually it climbs to a small cairn beyond which it

contours around the head of a valley on the right to reach another col **B** linking Winder with Arant Haw.

At the col, turn left having met up with another path. This now leads unerringly to the top of Winder, the summit marked by a triangulation pillar.

Leave the summit on the right-hand one of two ongoing grassy paths, which soon improves and eases steadily down the western ridge of Winder. Gradually, the descending path works down the side of the fell and comes to meet a wall not far from Nursery Wood. Turn right, alongside the wall for about 110 yds, where a metal gate will be found to give onto a rough surfaced, enclosed track. Go down this to a surfaced lane (Howgill Lane) **C**. Turn left, following the lane *and taking care against approaching traffic* as far as a stile beside a gate from where an ongoing footpath is signposted to Slacks Lane.

Go downfield beside a wall on the right, and a short way on passing above a stream gully to reach another stile beside a gate. Continue beyond this descending towards the buildings (mainly cottages/houses) at Underwinder, where another stile gives into house gardens, quickly crossed to another gate at the head of a surfaced lane. Head down the lane, later crossing a disused railway line, and following the lane down to a T-junction. Turn left to the main road (A684), and left again. *Take great care against approaching traffic*, and follow the road for 500 yds, as far as the entrance to Ingmire Hall **D**.

Here, leave the road by turning right onto a signposted bridleway for the A683. Continue past cottages and onto a delightful, enclosed path along the boundary of Ingmire Hall estate. The wooded track leads down to a rough surface, which in turn runs out to the A683. Turn right for about 110 yds, as far as a small lay-by on the left **E**, and there turn left through a metal kissing-gate (signposted to Birks Mill). Now following part of the Dales Way, head on to reach the banks of the River Rawthey, soon approaching the tiny settlement of Brigflatts.

The path runs between a fence and the river, but at a gate enters a large pasture. Keep on, parallel with the river, reaching an old railway viaduct. Go left through a gate and climb to cross the trackbed, descending steps on the other side to walk along the edge of another riverside pasture to a kissing-gate directly above the confluence of the rivers Dee and Rawthey **F**. The gate gives into a lightly wooded area before entering another riverside pasture. On

Brigflatts Brigflatts was once a flax weavers' settlement. Here stands a Friends' Meeting House, a small and beautiful white cottage, built as a co-operative effort in 1675, making it the oldest meeting house in the north of England. The house was built when non-conformist meetings were illegal, and failure to attend parish church brought persecution. It is said that one local man never attended the Meeting House services without taking his night cap against the possibility of being taken off to prison. One farmer, Alexander Hebblethwaite, was fined eight shillings for meeting here, an enormous sum, which he refused to pay, and forfeited his cow.

the far side, the path runs between a fence and the river, soon reaching the end of a surfaced lane near a small industrial site.

Keep forward along the lane, and continue past a group of cottages. Turn right onto the signposted Rawthey Way, which passes around a large house. As it does so, leave the obvious path, and go down towards the river, to gain, at a step-stile, the playing fields of Sedbergh School. Walk along the field edge, once more in company with the Rawthey.

Beyond the playing fields, the path eases briefly away from the river and climbs to a wall gap. From this go forward, keeping to the left of a ruined tower, and just beyond that, reaching the corner of woodland which, a short way farther on, it enters. The way through the wood is waymarked, and soon drops into a very narrow, walled passageway.

The path then continues above a steep drop to the river, and shortly leads to a gated gap-stile giving into a pasture, across which a path leads to the Sedbergh road. Turn left and walk into the village. ●

Bolton Abbey, Barden Tower and The Strid

walk 21

Start
Bolton Abbey

Distance
7½ miles (12km)

Height gain
1,035 feet (315m)

Approximate time
4 hours

Route terrain
Farmland; limestone moorland; riverside paths; woodland; and a little road walking

Parking
Bolton Abbey (Pay and Display)

OS maps
Landranger 104 (Leeds & Bradford), Explorer OL2 (Yorkshire Dales – Southern & Western areas)

GPS waypoints
SE 071 539
Ⓐ SE 072 542
Ⓑ SE 059 554
Ⓒ SE 043 554
Ⓓ SE 051 574

Bolton Abbey, or the remains thereof, have been the inspiration of many – poets, artists, photographers and authors generally. The ruins harmonise well with their setting amid meadow, moorland, woodland and the sinuous embrace of the River Wharfe, creating a scene of unrivalled beauty. A short distance up river, the Wharfe barges its way through a narrow rocky gorge, The Strid, while farther on it passes the ruins of Barden Tower. All these elements combine in this walk, which begins with a steady ascent onto moorland before heading for the river.

The first part of the walk, across fields, woods and moorland, is easy to follow. From the car park walk out to the Burnsall road and turn left, and, soon after passing beneath an 18th-century arch (that was once an aqueduct), branch left onto a track signposted to Halton Heights Ⓐ.

Follow the track for a short distance to a gate, and here bear right and across a field to a footpath sign near a fence corner and a pond. Follow the fence, and then cross to a gate, turning right in the ensuing field, stepping across a mid-field stream, to enter a wood. After a short climb, turn abruptly left at a signpost, and follow the ongoing path through the wood to a gate in a wall.

Now strike across the ensuing field to a gate in a wall, and from it maintain a similar direction, heading across another large pasture and aiming for another gate about 30 yds to the east of a wall corner Ⓑ.

Through the gate, turn left to follow a path parallel with a wall on the left to the col between Little and Middle Hare Head, where the path rises onto the latter. Continue across this minor summit to a gate in a wall, and a few strides farther on, leave the main path by branching right Ⓒ to descend through heather and then bracken to a gate beside the road below. Ignore the gate, but continue alongside the wall to another gate lower down, just above a wall corner. Through this, turn right and follow the road to a T-junction with the B6160. There turn left and walk down to Barden Tower.

From the tower, leave the B6160 by branching right down the

Barden Tower Barden Tower used to belong to the Clifford family, whose main stronghold was Skipton Castle. It was originally built in the 12th century as a hunting lodge, but was rebuilt and extended in the 15th century, and it is the ruins of this later building that remain today.

road for Appletreewick, walking as far as Barden Bridge and, just before the bridge **D**, turn right, through a wall gap and down steps to join a riverside path. The remaining section, largely shared with the Dales Way, simply follows the river and is quite delightful.

Shortly after passing a turreted bridge – a Victorian aqueduct carrying water to Bradford – keep on across meadows to a gate giving into Strid Woods. The woodland is owned by the Devonshire Estates and a small charge is usually levied to walk through them.

Although there are a number of paths through the woodland – and with time you could easily explore more – this walk follows the path closest to the river. *During wet conditions some parts of the path can be slippery.*

Eventually, the path reaches the narrowing known as The Strid, where the cascading water is usually heard long before it is seen. At one point here the river is only a few yards wide and surges through the gap with tremendous force: *this is not a place to attempt any heroics by trying to leap across the river – quite a few people have died here hoping to do just that.*

Strid Wood is renowned for its flora and fauna. Almost all of the trees are broad-leaved, some as much as 300 years old. There are at least 60 species of nesting birds here and over 80 species of lichen.

After The Strid the path is a little easier, and broadens out into a flat and well-defined track that eventually

Bolton Abbey

works a way onward to Cavendish Pavilion, beside which the river is crossed by a footbridge. On the other side, turn right to a stile and there turn left by Pickles Beck. Cross a minor road (Hazlewood Lane) and walk uphill for a short distance to a signposted path on the right for Bolton Abbey.

The path winds agreeably through riverside woodland, eventually dropping to a broad grassy expanse formed by a river loop. Ahead lies another Wharfe bridge, beyond which stand the ruins of Bolton Priory. Across the bridge

follow a clear path up to a flight of steps leading up to a 'hole' in a wall. *Take care emerging onto the road beyond.* Cross with care and go ahead to return to the visitor centre and car park. ●

> **Bolton Priory**   Bolton Priory was founded in 1154 and dissolved in 1539, one of the last among Henry VIII's Dissolution of the Monasteries to fall. Part of the structure, however, survives and is still used as the local church. The surrounding priory buildings have almost entirely disappeared, apart from the gatehouse, which is incorporated into the present, mainly Victorian, Bolton Hall.

SCALE 1:25000 or 2½ INCHES to 1 MILE 4CM to 1KM

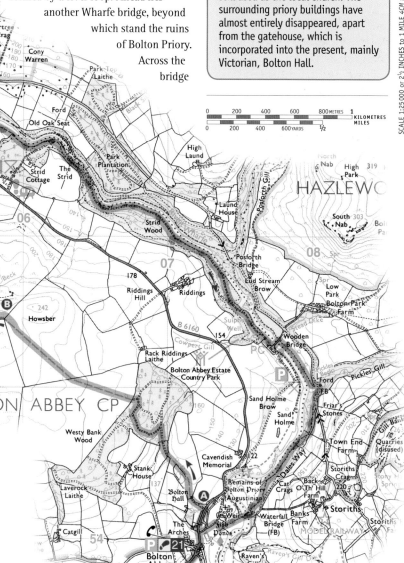

Giggleswick Scar and Stainforth Force

Start
Settle

Distance
8½ miles (13.5km)

Height gain
1,245 feet (380m)

Approximate time
4½ hours

Route terrain
Farmland; limestone moorland; a little road walking; riverside paths

P Parking
Settle (Pay and Display)

OS maps
Landranger 98 (Wensleydale & Upper Wharfedale), Explorer OL41 (Forest of Bowland & Ribblesdale)

GPS waypoints
SD 819 638
Ⓐ SD 813 640
Ⓑ SD 808 653
Ⓒ SD 790 676
Ⓓ SD 817 672

From the busy market town of Settle, the walk first climbs onto Giggleswick Scar before cutting across wild and open limestone moorland to the isolated hamlet of Feizor. The return leg explores yet more wide open spaces before dropping to Little Stainforth and the banks of the River Ribble. Stainforth Force provides a spectacular white water moment before the river relaxes and offers companionship all the way back to Settle.

Settle Like most larger market towns in the Dales, Settle lies on a river, the Ribble in this case, at a point where the narrow uplands of the dale broaden into a wider and greener valley. The Ribble, unlike most Dales' rivers, flows west into the Irish Sea instead of east to the North Sea. The town is a delightful mix of winding streets and small squares, and makes an excellent walking centre.

Leave the centre of Settle by turning down a pedestrianised side street opposite the town hall (signposted for the Friends' Meeting House), and go ahead beneath the railway line and forward past a supermarket, walking on as far as the fire station. Just before the fire station, turn left onto a surfaced pathway between a light industrial estate and housing. At the bottom of the pathway, bear right, passing around converted warehouses to locate a footbridge spanning the Ribble.

Cross the bridge, and bear half-left, uphill to a gate giving onto a walled passageway that emerges at the edge of Giggleswick. Turn right and walk to the end of Bankwell Road, there turning right and climbing steeply (Belle Hill) to meet the main road. Cross into The Mains opposite Ⓐ.

At the top end of The Mains, leave the housing behind by going forward onto an enclosed path, that wanders on easily and finally climbs to the upper edge of woodland at a ladder-stile.

Over the stile, turn immediately right on a path roughly parallel with a wall. After about 110 yds, as the path forks, branch left, climbing across rough ground to run alongside the upper edge of a huge quarry. Keep on to pass the quarry, and then, beyond it, bear left, heading for a waymark pole and, farther on, a signpost. At the signpost Ⓑ, bear right onto a

SCALE 1:27 777 or 2¼ INCHES to 1 MILE 3.6CM to 1KM

lovely path that goes forward along the edge of Giggleswick Scar.

After a wall gap, the path bears left, keeping below the uppermost level of the Scar. The path leads on to a ladder-stile and then continues to another about 330 yds distant. Over the second of these, keep forward on a clear path, roughly parallel with a wall at the escarpment edge. The path leads to a gate and finger-post. Beyond, bear half-right on a clear path heading out onto the limestone plateau.

The path takes a clear route across the plateau, linked by gates and ladder-stiles, and continues to another finger-post at the high point of the route, beyond which it descends as a broad grassy track to Feizor, there reaching a gate at the edge of the hamlet.

Go through the gate and down to a surfaced lane, turning right, following the road for a short distance before turning right over a ladder-stile **C**. Go forward (signposted for Stainforth) to a small gate and then keep ahead up a shallow rocky gully, and continuing along the right-hand side of a pasture, beside a wall. Just before the end of the field, cross another ladder-stile, and bear left, climbing gently.

The path rises steadily to a high point from which it heads forward across limestone moorland, on a broad grassy track, with the route clear throughout and linked by ladder-stiles.

The track offers lovely views of Ribblesdale and eventually descends to a gate just above Little Stainforth. Go down towards the buildings below, and on to a crossroads. Keep forward, and soon reach Stainforth Bridge **D**, an attractive packhorse bridge built in the 17th century.

Leave the road here by turning through a gap-stile to reach the true right bank of the Ribble, with the spectacular Stainforth Force only a short way ahead.

A clear path now parallels the river at varying distances from it, and continuing very agreeably as far as a footbridge. Here, ignore the bridge, and turn right up a walled lane to Stackhouse. At a T-junction, turn left along a lane, following this as far as a signposted gap-stile on the left, *and taking care against approaching traffic.*

Cross a field, and then resume a course much nearer to the river, gradually losing height until finally, at the edge of a playing field, the path once more touches upon the riverbank. A path now runs along the edge of the playing field to meet the main road at the edge of Settle. Turn left and walk back into town.

On the moors above Feizor

Semer Water

walk 23

Start
Bainbridge

Distance
8½ miles (13.5km)

Height gain
1,395 feet (425m)

Approximate time
4½ hours

Route terrain
Riverside paths; farmland; moorland; some road walking

Parking
Around Bainbridge village green

OS maps
Landranger 98 (Wensleydale & Upper Wharfedale), Explorer OL30 (Yorkshire Dales – Northern & Central areas)

GPS waypoints
SD 934 902
Ⓐ SD 921 877
Ⓑ SD 912 878
Ⓒ SD 885 872
Ⓓ SD 905 883

Semer Water, one of only two natural lakes in the Yorkshire Dales, is surrounded by moors and thinly populated farmland. The lake itself is of modest size, but its setting is perfect, possessing an air of mystery and quiet intrigue. Beginning in the village of Bainbridge, this agreeable walk wanders easily across hillsides above the River Bain to the spread of Semer Water, before heading onto the moors to join a Roman road for the final stage back to Bainbridge.

Bainbridge Bainbridge is arguably the most attractive village in Wensleydale, and developed as a base for foresters. Until fairly recently, the custom of blowing a forest horn each evening – as a guide to travellers in the forest – was still carried on, but, like so many ancient customs, has fallen from grace. The origins of the tradition are rooted in Saxon times, when the dalesfolk blew a horn to warn of danger or to instigate a hue and cry against poachers. In Norman times, strangers entering what had become the royal hunting Forest of Wensleydale, wolf-infested and overrun with deer and wild boar, were obliged to blow a horn to show they came with peaceful intent. Around Semer Water, a horn was sounded whenever a wolf was spotted near the isolated 'setts' so that the animals could be herded to safety. When the last wolf was killed in Britain, the horn was still a signal to the farmers to move their livestock to fresh pastures.

Begin from the village green in Bainbridge by heading out in the Leyburn direction. After a short uphill stroll, leave the road just by a lay-by turning onto a path on the right signposted to Semer Water. The path climbs and shortly runs alongside a wall before branching across hillside pastures on a footpath that leads ultimately to a wall with two, gated gap-stiles. Take the stile on the right and follow a green path over a slight rise before descending to a wall corner. Then follow a path running beside the wall. Cross more hill pastures and descend to a ladder-stile. Having crossed the stile, follow a green path beside the River Bain to reach Semer Water Bridge Ⓐ.

Go over the bridge, as if heading to nearby Countersett, and in a few strides leave the road for a footpath on the left signposted to Marsett Lane. The path crosses a number of fields to meet the lane at a step-stile. Turn left and follow the lane for

Semer Water   Semer Water is a product of the last ice age, formed by morainic debris which effectively dammed the whole valley. The lake is today only a shadow of its former self, but the river provides an interesting geological snippet. Unlike conventional rivers, the River Bain is blocked in its upper reaches by glacial drift. This has the effect of increasing the gradient lower down. So, the river starts off with a gentle gradient, becoming more energetic as it passes through the dale, and cutting through rock before finally producing waterfalls on the outskirts of Bainbridge.

The geological explanation of how the valley, known as Raydale, was formed is rather prosaic. Legend provides a more intriguing account. Here, it is said, an angel came one day disguised as a beggar, seeking food and shelter, but was turned away by everyone in the village, until, at last, the angel came to a ramshackle hut set a distance from the rest. Here the stranger was invited in to share the meagre possessions of the man and his wife who lived there. The next morning, the angel, being in an uncharacteristically vengeful mood, turned towards the village below, and brought forth great torrents from the hillsides that flooded the village and drowned all its inhabitants, save for the man and his wife. Just along the road from Semer Water Bridge stands Low Blean, said to be the house of the hospitable couple.

about 550 yds as far as a footpath (a broad farm track) on the right for Countersett and Cragg Side Road.

Turn onto the track and walk ahead past barns to a gate and stile. In the next pasture, climb (steeply and trackless) obliquely right to another stile in the top right-hand corner of the pasture. From there, head diagonally right, up-field towards a powerline pole near a wall corner, and then continue climbing, crossing walls, until you can climb a final pasture to a ladder-stile giving onto Cragg Side Road **B**.

Immediately leave the road through a gate on the left to pursue a broad track (signposted to Wether Fell). Follow the rising track to a gate and through this bear left to another gate, and then rising beyond on a green track.

The track leads up onto the moorland top and forward through two gates/ stiles, pressing on across the moor to intersect a footpath (signposted), near which another signpost points the way forward to the 'Roman road'. Keep on in the same direction to meet the broad, stony track of Cam High

SCALE 1:25 000 or 2½ INCHES to 1 MILE 4CM to 1KM

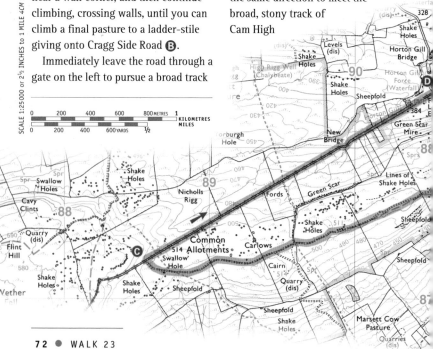

Road **C**, the Roman road between Ingleton and Bainbridge. At the road, turn right and walk in the footsteps of legionnaires all the way back to the outskirts of Bainbridge. At Four Lane Ends **D** cross the surfaced road linking Burtersett and Countersett. Beyond, Cam High Road sweeps on downhill across Bainbridge High Pasture to rejoin the Countersett road on the edge of Bainbridge. Now simply follow the surfaced road down into Bainbridge.

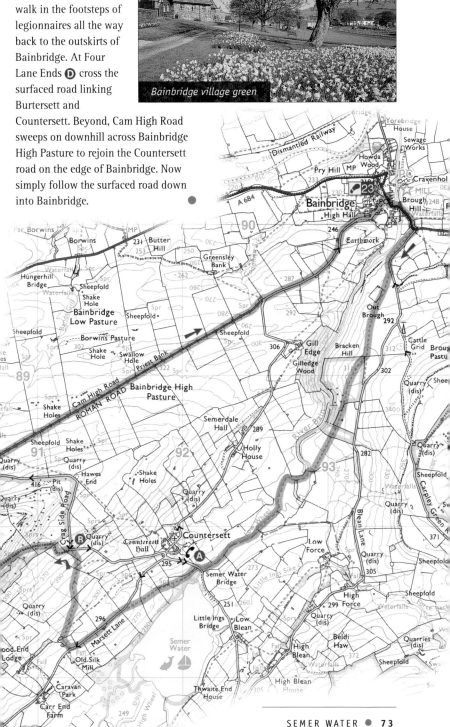

Bainbridge village green

walk 24

Start
Pateley Bridge

Distance
9 miles (14.5km)

Height gain
1,245 feet (380m)

Approximate time
4½ hours

Route terrain
Farmland; moorland; riverside paths and a little road walking

Parking
Pateley Bridge (Pay and Display)

OS maps
Landranger 99 (Northallerton & Ripon), Explorer 298 (Nidderdale)

GPS waypoints
- SE 157 655
- Ⓐ SE 175 651
- Ⓑ SE 192 654
- Ⓒ SE 210 655
- Ⓓ SE 208 640
- Ⓔ SE 192 642
- Ⓕ SE 188 638

Pateley Bridge and Brimham Rocks

This delightful walk takes an elevated route out of Pateley Bridge, offering lovely views as it heads towards Brimham Rocks. From the rocks, the walk heads for Smelthouses, eventually reaching the River Nidd, alongside which it returns to the start.

Nidderdale Of all the Dales, Nidderdale is the least well-known nationally – though local walkers have enjoyed its pleasures for years. It was excluded from the Yorkshire Dales National Park, but did later receive some protection when it was created an Area of Outstanding Natural Beauty. Pateley Bridge, where this walk begins, is a busy Dales town on the banks of the River Nidd, and gets its name from the river crossing first used by the monks of Fountains Abbey. Lead mining, quarrying and to a lesser extent textiles were all important in the history of Pateley Bridge, though today the economy is largely based on agriculture and tourism.

Leave Pateley Bridge by walking up High Street and at the top turning right with the main road into Ripon Road to go past the Methodist church. A short way farther on, leave the road by turning left up steps onto the signposted Panorama

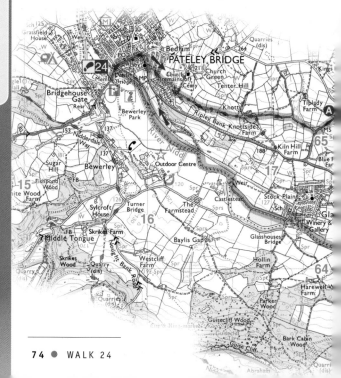

Brimham Rocks

Walk. A surfaced path climbs between walls, with steadily improving views across the dale, until it reaches a road at Bishopdale House. Here, keep left, still climbing between walls to another junction, where road surfacing begins. Keep forward, now descending gently, the route signposted for Blazefield.

As the road bends right 110 yds farther on, leave it by branching left onto a vehicle track (signposted as the Nidderdale Way). After passing a cottage the track deteriorates to an overgrown path. When it forks, bear right, descending and eventually emerging at a road. Turn left and walk

up towards the terraced houses of Blazefield.

After about 220 yds, as the first houses are reached, leave the road by branching right onto a continuation of the Nidderdale Way **Ⓐ**, which runs along the terrace, and then starts to descend as a rough vehicle track. With the added height gain since leaving Pateley Bridge, the view across the dale is even better.

At a minor road, turn right, leaving the Nidderdale Way and descending for about 110 yds to a signposted path on the left for Wilsill. Turn left here, through two metal gates and then from a third gate keep forward across a grassy slope, and later bearing left to a wooden gate in a field corner. Through the gate keep forward through another and along the top edge of two sloping pastures, walking beside a wall to a final gate giving onto a lane at Raikes.

SCALE 1:29,412 or 2⅛ INCHES to 1 MILE 3.4CM to 1KM

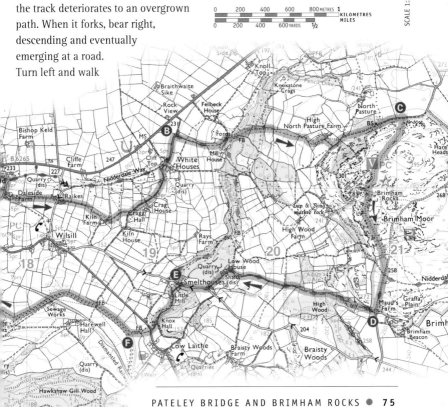

Cross into a narrow, enclosed path opposite sandwiched between buildings, and soon reach a step-stile from which keep forward to a wall gap, and then cross to a gate. Shortly, beyond the gate (and just before the next one), a stile on the right crosses into the adjacent field. Then go half left to a gate, and continue across the next field following a wall on the right to a gate, just beside a cottage. Cross in front of the cottage to a narrow gap-stile and wooden gate, and then bear left alongside a wall to a wall junction. Maintain the same direction, going forward towards light woodland and a metal gate in a field corner.

Through the gate, turn left onto a rough track, and immediately left again onto a waymarked bridleway between overgrown walls. Continue to a track junction at White Houses and then go forward onto a bridleway signposted for Ripon Road, having now rejoined the Nidderdale Way. Keep going as far as a row of cottages and a signposted footpath on the right for Brimham Rocks **B** just before the first cottage. Turn right here along an enclosed path to a stile.

The ongoing route downfield is waymarked and provides a fine view across to Brimham Rocks. It leads through a wall gap to a vehicle track. Go left to a track junction just at the edge of the wooded gorge that contains Fell Beck. From the junction bear right on a waymarked footpath that leads to a footbridge spanning the beck.

From the footbridge, cross a stile and follow a track beside a fence, climbing steadily and generally keeping to the left-hand edge of a number of fields. Eventually, on reaching a narrow field end with North Pasture Farm in view ahead, keep to the right-hand wall as it

Brimham Rocks

bends right, to locate a small ladder-stile. Cross the next field to a step-stile, and then take to the farm access for a short while. Stick with the access as it runs on through light woodland.

The ongoing track climbs gently, and just after the high point , leave it to fight a way through trackless heather and bracken to reach the northern edge of moorland wherein sit the Brimham Rocks.

There are many paths across the moorland, and which you take is irrelevant – the general direction is south-west, but time should be taken to explore this fantastic landscape. The rocks are a series of gritstone boulders, fashioned by time and weather into shapes that have inevitably attracted fanciful names from Victorian visitors – the Dancing Bear, the Anvil, the Sphinx. This whole area is owned by the

National Trust, who have provided an information centre, shop, and car park, and it is the car park which eventually becomes the objective. From it begins the return journey to Pateley Bridge.

Walk out from the car park and swing left to a T-junction and there turn right along a surfaced lane for about 330 yds, as far as a signpost ⓓ for Smelthouses. Take the right-hand one of two gates ahead and follow a grassy path below a low cliff which winds attractively downhill through woodland and across fields towards Low Wood House. Here bear left to reach a road, and turn right towards Smelthouses.

On reaching Smelthouses, turn left ⓔ, just before Fell Beck bridge onto a signposted bridleway, a stony track that leads past old mill buildings converted to houses and soon rejoins Fell Beck as it passes along the edge of more light woodland. The track comes down to pass through another group of buildings to reach the road at Low Laithe.

Cross onto a path opposite signposted for Glasshouses and follow a field path to a wall corner where a stile gives onto a narrow path leading to a footbridge for the last crossing of Fell Beck. A short distance farther on, Fell Beck meets its confluence with the River Nidd ⓕ.

Turn right to walk up-river, crossing an in-flowing stream on stepping stones. With only minor deviations, keep going until the path is deflected right through a small light industrial estate at Glasshouses.

Emerging at a road, turn left and just before reaching the Nidd bridge, turn right onto a signposted path, a broad track between low walls that soon reaches a large reservoir. The track continues past a weir, and then becomes a surfaced path along the banks of the river, leading unerringly back into Pateley Bridge. ●

walk 25

Start

Ingleton

Distance

8 miles (13km)

Height gain

2,035 feet (620m)

Approximate time

5 hours

Route terrain

Farmland; mountain moorland; road walking

Parking

Village centre (Pay and Display)

OS maps

Landranger 98 (Wensleydale & Upper Wharfedale), Explorer OL2 (Yorkshire Dales – Southern & Western areas)

GPS waypoints

SD 695 730
Ⓐ SD 701 731
Ⓑ SD 722 734
Ⓒ SD 742 737
Ⓓ SD 720 714

Ingleborough from Ingleton

Viewed from the southwest, Ingleborough rises as an isolated summit from an extensive plateau of limestone culminating in a fine series of scars overlooking Chapel-le-Dale, and rising through 1,870ft (570m). Once thought to have been the highest summit in England, the mountain has a unique appeal, its great sprawl dominating the countryside of West Craven, its distinctive flat-topped summit a feature easily identifiable from as far away as the western fells of Lakeland.

Begin from the main car park in Ingleton and walk out to the Hawes road, there turning left and, *taking care against approaching traffic,* walk up the road as it leaves the village. As it reaches Fell End, hill slopes appear on the right, and here you can leave the road by branching right onto a broad vehicle track Ⓐ (Fell Lane) that serves Crina Bottom Farm. At first the track climbs steadily, but then levels as it enters a walled section, just as Ingleborough and more distant Whernside come briefly into view. Off to the left (north-west) a long ridge leads over Gragareth, the highest point in Lancashire.

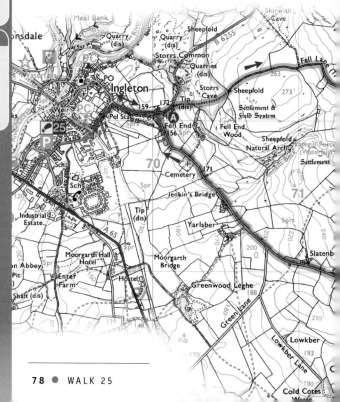

Ingleton

Ingleton is a delightful place with a history that reaches back to the Iron Age, when a fortress was built on the summit of Ingleborough. More recently the village economy was founded on quarrying and coal mining.

Ingleton boasts the first Hoffman kiln, a type of kiln principally used in brick making, which gives a continuous operation. It is still visible in Meal Bank quarry on the northern banks of the River Doe. Cotton mills were once plentiful here, powered by a water mill, of which there is now little trace, although traces of the mill races are still to be found near the river.

There are also some fine 16th-century buildings in Ingleton, and remnants of an agricultural past, notably the old bullring where animals were baited and slaughtered in bygone years. The Church of St Mary houses one of Ingleton's oldest relics, a Norman font, salvaged from the river. Mary Doyle, the mother of Sir Arthur Conan Doyle, used to live in nearby Masongill, a small hamlet to the north west, and Doyle himself would doubtless have been a regular visitor to the area.

Simply follow the walled lane as it bends around White Scars, and finally comes to an end at a gate.

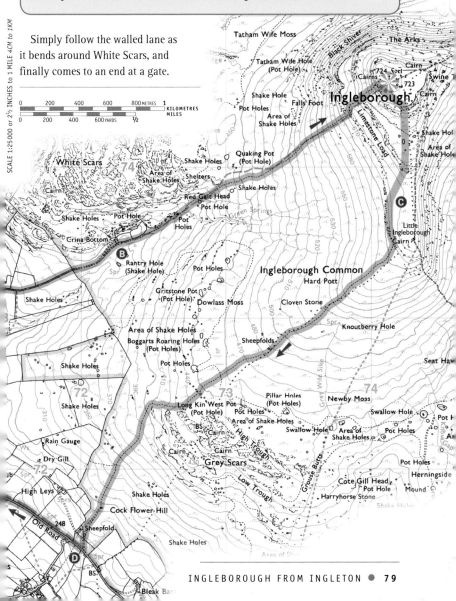

> **Ingleborough** Based on a thick layer of limestone, the mountain and its moorland surrounds are a repeated succession of shales, limestones and sandstones – the Yoredale Facies – capped by a resilient layer of millstone grit. Twenty thousand years ago a deep covering of glacial ice gouged out the features we see today, while meltwater rivers carved valleys and gorges in the still frozen landscape. Then, as the climate changed, and the caves became unblocked, rivers sank underground into the heart of this classic karst country. It is this treasury of geological history that gives Ingleborough its distinctive profile and its claim to fame.

Ingleborough is now clearly in view directly ahead, and looking a little daunting viewed end on as it is.

A short way farther on beyond the gate the track forks. Here, branch right, descending a little to pass below Crina Bottom Farm **B**, an isolated farmstead. As you pass the farm, the path continues clearly enough and undulates across in-flowing streams before finally getting to grips with the pull up Ingleborough's flank. Taken steadily, the ascent is not so tiring as might be supposed. Nearing the summit, you pass across one of the distinctive 'lips' that give Ingleborough such a shapely outline. Beyond, a little more ascent awaits.

As you reach the rim you pass through the remains of a hillfort wall, a massive encircling wall, now collapsed, around the edge of a summit plateau which also contains the foundations, still traceable in the peaty summit, of 19 circular huts believed to be a settlement of the first Iron Age man in this district.

The summit, a massive cairn, is nearby. It stands beside a trig point and a crossed-wall shelter surmounted by a view indicator and erected by the Ingleton Fell and Rescue Team to commemorate the Coronation of Queen Elizabeth in 1953. The highest point, the true summit, is marked by a cairn on a rocky plinth a few metres northwest of the trig, and overlooks the Doe valley and the long trail of your ascent. The plinth has a history of its own, being the site of a round tower (a hospice) built in 1830, but substantially destroyed on the day of its opening by participants rather the worse for drink: the curved stones which formed its base are still clearly seen.

Leave Ingleborough summit heading south-east to the edge of the summit plateau, and there pass through the remains of the hill fort. This is the route from Clapham, but the route across the summit plateau path is not easily discernible in poor visibility. From the plateau rim, follow the track down, as if heading for Little Ingleborough, but on reaching level ground, leave the path **C** before Little Ingleborough and bear right (i.e. west) to overlook Ingleborough Common. Before long a clear grassy track comes into view, overgrown in a few places. It runs south, briefly, and then wanders down across the common towards a feature known as the Cloven Stone (which is easily missed).

The path is marked on the current map, and for the most part is easy enough to follow. The objective is an area of limestone known as Grey Scars, where there are quite a few pot holes. Beyond Grey Scars the ground drops a little more steeply as it heads down to a track leading down to the Old Road between Newby Cote and Ingleton **D**.

On reaching the road, turn right and follow the road for just over one mile back to Ingleton. The road is still used by traffic, but is much less busy than of old. ●

Nine Standards Rigg

walk 26

 Start
Kirkby Stephen
Market Place

Distance
9 miles (14.5km)

 Height gain
1,770 feet (540m)

Approximate time
5 hours

Route terrain
Mainly minor roads
and moorland tracks,
but also some boggy
stretches

P **Parking**
On-street parking and
parking areas

 OS maps
Landranger 91
(Appleby-in-
Westmorland), Explorer
OL19 (Howgills &
Upper Eden Valley)

GPS waypoints
NY 775 087
Ⓐ NY 783 086
Ⓑ NY 810 067
Ⓒ NY 827 057
Ⓓ NY 817 058

Although this walk spends most of its time in Cumbria, it climbs through 1,722 ft (525m) to a significant vantage point on the very edge of the Yorkshire Dales, the watershed of the gathering grounds of the River Swale. The Nine Standards are a familiar sight to the people of Kirkby Stephen, and to anyone undertaking the Coast-to-Coast walk, which passes this way. They make a fine and airy objective for a walk, enjoyed by many. Most walkers satisfy themselves with simply going up to the Nine Standards, and then retreating, but this walk attempts a short, boggy loop across the high peat moorland, where the skills of navigation are needed. You may not want to tackle the extension after prolonged wet weather!

Leave the Market Place (opposite the **Pennine Hotel**) by a short lane to the right of the entrance to the churchyard. Pass public conveniences, and descend Stoneshot bearing right, and then left down steps, to meet the River Eden at Frank's Bridge.

The River Eden finds its source high up on the slopes of Mallerstang, on Black Fell Moss, not far, in fact, from the birthplace of the Ure and the Swale.

Cross Frank's Bridge, where an ever-present assembly of ducks greets walkers with a chorus of appeals for food. Turn right to follow the river for a short distance until it swings away, right, and then, from a metal kissing-gate, follow a surfaced path ahead beside a wall and later a laid hedgerow to another gate in the top left corner of the field. Through this go forward along an enclosed path to enter the hamlet of Hartley **Ⓐ**.

On reaching a road, cross diagonally left to a narrow path leading to a small bridge spanning Hartley Beck. Another road awaits; this time turn right. When the road swings left a short way farther on, you can go with it, or leave it on the apex by going forward to the right of a garage to engage a brief but lovely wooded interlude, a path that clings to Hartley Beck a while longer before rejoining the road. Turn right again, and now climb steadily to reach the entrance to Hartley Quarry.

Here swing left, still climbing, and continue with the fell road, which affords fine retrospective views across the Vale of Eden to the high Pennine summits of Cross Fell and Great Dun Fell. A short descent takes you past the entrance to Fell House Farm, a rather isolated outpost, beyond which you climb once more to the road end. Just past the road end, take the left

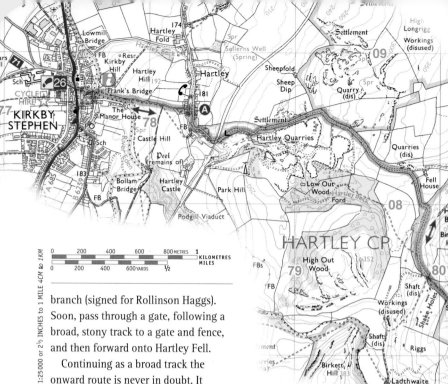

SCALE 1:25000 or 2½ INCHES to 1 MILE 4CM to 1KM

branch (signed for Rollinson Haggs). Soon, pass through a gate, following a broad, stony track to a gate and fence, and then forward onto Hartley Fell.

Continuing as a broad track the onward route is never in doubt. It crosses Faraday Gill where sedimentary rocks and shales have been exposed on the left, and soon joins company with a wall (on the right). Before long the wall bears south-east and then south with Faraday Gill on the left as it flows down from the slopes of Nine Standards Rigg.

> **Faraday Gill** Faraday Gill, commemorates the local family whose offspring, Michael (1791-1867), was the physicist who discovered electromagnetic induction and other important electrical and magnetic phenomena.

Continue for a short distance to a signpost pointing the way up on to Nine Standards Rigg **B**. Thus far the route has followed the Coast-to-Coast walk, and continues to do so, but the section up on to Nine Standards Rigg has been greatly improved in recent years. Now a broad, clear path leads unerringly up to the renovated monoliths on the summit ridge.

The highest point of Nine Standards Rigg occurs at the trig point, a short way to the south, beyond a viewpoint indicator.

The onward route lies beyond the trig point, but for a while the going is free range and very rough, across heather and tussock grass moorland, and with innumerable peat bogs to circumvent and no path to follow. So, *if this is not for you, simply retrace your outward route from the Nine Standards – the continuing route does, in any case, rejoin the outward route at the foot of Faraday Gill.*

But if there is adventure in your soul – and it is a clear day, and you can navigate across untracked moorland, and do not mind a bit of floundering in bog (Coast-to-Coast walkers have to come this way anyway) – then continue past the trig, descending to an extensive boggy area on the very edge of the

Descending from Nine Standards Rigg

Yorkshire Dales National Park **C**. The Coast-to-Coast route turns left here, for Whitsundale – once it escapes the clutches of the peat. But this walk turns right, to the west. There is no path for quite some time, and no real sense of direction, except west. Do not be lured by a large, conspicuous cairn to the south-west; keep north of this. You will have a wonderful time evading peat patrols waiting to ambush you, and

achieve a fine sense of achievement in doing so.

Eventually, by maintaining that westerly course from point **C** you pass some scattered rocky outcrops and a wide grassy channel through the peat (Rollinson Haggs), and reach another signpost on the line of a bad weather route for the Coast-to-Coast **D**. Keep

Nine Standards Rigg Arrival at the Nine Standards is a moment of some occasion: it lies on the watershed of Britain, that great north-south divide sending waters one way to the Irish Sea, and the other to the North Sea, although there are times and rainy days when you gain the distinct impression its sends them nowhere at all.

No one has yet come up with any historical fact about the origins or purpose of the Nine Standards. Over a period of time they had fallen into disrepair, but in recent years they have been completely and magnificently restored. They stand on the former county boundary between Westmorland and the North Riding of Yorkshire, and, more than likely, their origin derives from that significance, though one fanciful notion suggests they were built to persuade marauding Scots that an English army was camped up there, which as Neil Hanson points out in Walking through Eden 'suggests a contempt for Scottish intelligence that even the English would find hard to maintain.'

On a clear and fine day there are few places that give a wider, more inspiring, panorama of the massive sprawling beauty of the wild moorlands of Northern England than Nine Standards. It is one of the most far-reaching views extending from the mounds of Cross Fell, the Dun Fells and Mickle Fell in the north to the lofty escarpment of Wild Boar Fell across the upper Vale of Eden.

ahead here, contouring across the moorland shoulder in a north-westerly direction, high above Dukerdale. For a while the path is not very clear, but steadily improves, and, as you head down towards a wall, becomes a wide grassy track. Turn right along it and, free of all bogs and tough going, rejoin the outward route below Faraday Gill, and then simply retrace your steps. ●

Nine Standards

Ingleborough from Clapham

walk 27

Start
Clapham

Distance
10½ miles (17km)

Height gain
2,230 feet (680m)

Approximate time
5½ hours

Route terrain
Good tracks and upland paths; mainly across limestone

Parking
Clapham (Pay and Display)

O S maps
Landranger 98 (Wensleydale & Upper Wharfedale), Explorer OL2 (Yorkshire Dales – Southern & Western areas)

GPS waypoints
- SD 745 692
- Ⓐ SD 752 708
- Ⓑ SD 752 723
- Ⓒ SD 766 739
- Ⓓ SD 775 731
- Ⓔ SD 758 716

A fine walk of no great difficulty (unless you fall into Gaping Gill!) beginning in a charming village, and taking in meltwater ravines, potholes, wild moorland wandering, a high mountain summit, and dramatic limestone scenery. There are other ascents of Ingleborough, but this is undoubtedly the best.

Clapham is a village of rare delight, captivating at every turn of the road, tastefully decorated with old bridges and waterfalls, white cottages, old stone houses and stands of ancient trees. It is a place of which 'rural charm' is not so much a cliché as a way of life, a place with a comfortable atmosphere of peace and tranquility. Weekends, as happens throughout the Yorkshire Dales, inject an element of fretting and fraying as visitors trip in to revitalise their jaded weekday spirits.

Viewed from the south west, Ingleborough rises as an isolated summit from an extensive plateau of limestone culminating in a fine series of scars overlooking Chapel-le-Dale. Once thought to have been the highest summit in England, the mountain has a unique appeal, its great sprawl dominating the countryside of west Craven, its distinctive flat-topped summit a feature easily identifiable from as far away as the western fells of Lakeland. Unspectacular in mountaineering terms, the vast Ingleborough landscape is nonetheless remarkable, its diverse nooks and crannies an immense store of botanical and archaeological goodies, its geological infrastructure a honeycomb of delight.

On leaving the car park, turn right and soon go left to cross Clapham Beck by an old stone bridge. Turn right and shortly pause for a moment to take in the lovely Clapham Falls. When the road swings to the left, follow it for a short distance until you can turn right into Clapdale Lane (signed: 'Ingleborough; Gaping Gill; Ingleborough Cave'). For a while the lane is surfaced, climbing steadily until it runs on as a rough track to Clapdale Farm. Go forward through the farmyard, and on the other side immediately descend, right, following a clear path towards Clapham Beck Ⓐ. Through a gate turn left, heading upstream to arrive at the entrance to Ingleborough Cave.

Continue past the cave, and through a sheltered glen between low scars of limestone. Ahead, the main valley curves to the left and a stile gives into the rocky

Ingleborough Cave

In the early years of the 19th century the underground network of caverns between Gaping Gill and Clapham Beck Head remained a source of mystery and wonder. Ingleborough Cave, the obvious entrance, was blocked after only a few metres by a wall of stalagmite beyond which a tiny space of air stretched above a pool of water into the darkness. Occasional floods suggested that this cave might be connected to the underground river of Gaping Gill, and so in 1837 the landowner ordered the stalagmite barrier to be broken down, to drain away the lake it held back, and to allow exploration of the interior. A fine cavern was found part of the way to Gaping Gill, but it took almost another 150 years of spasmodic exploration before the final link was made.

Open: daily, 10.00–16.00, Feb–Oct; weekends all year. Tours on the hour. Entrance fee. Tel. 01524 251242 www.ingleboroughcave.co.uk

maw of Trow Gill, a classic example of a limestone gorge, built by a surface stream of meltwater flowing off the limestone plateau above as the glaciers retreated at the end of the last ice age. Rising steadily

Labels on map: Pot Holes · Caves · Fell Close · Cave · Pot Hole · Cave · Areas of Shake Holes · Shake Holes · Cairn · Cave · Area of Shake Holes · Grouse Butts · Shooting Hut · Grouse Butts · The Allotment · Nick Pot · Sulber Pot · Settlement & Field System · Pot Holes · Grouse Butts · Pile of Stones · Sulber · Juniper Gulf · Sulber Gate · Thieves Moss · Pot Holes · Area of Shake Holes · Shake Hole · Beggar's Stile Cairn · Shake Hole · Pile of Stones · Pot Holes · Settlement · Area of Shake Holes · Area of Shake Holes · Crummack Dale · Long Scar · Rain Gauge · Cairn · Cave · Crumm

SCALE 1:27777 or 2¼ INCHES to 1 MILE 3.6CM to 1KM

0 200 400 600 800 METRES 1 KILOMETRES MILES
0 200 400 600 YARDS ½

Gaping Gill

Gaping Gill takes its name from its great entrance, which swallows with ease the waters of Fell Beck as they gather from the high grounds of Ingleborough. This wide open hole, of obviously great depth, was an irresistible challenge to the explorers of the 19th century, but it was not until the last decade of the century that a Frenchman, Edouard Martel, in August 1895, finally reached the floor of the shaft, more than 300ft (100m) down. The main chamber of Gaping Gill is the largest cavern in Britain, 460ft (140m) long and almost 100ft (30m) high and wide.

the gorge is overlooked by slopes becoming higher and steeper, until it narrows dramatically to a spill of boulders over which walkers must clamber to reach the dry, grassy valley beyond.

The path now follows the line of a wall to a couple of adjacent ladder-stiles **B** (ignore an earlier single stile), beyond which lies the broad limestone plinth of Ingleborough. The onward route is now obvious. When the path forks, bear right to visit Gaping Gill.

From Gaping Gill a path heads north west for the base of Little Ingleborough which is gained by a steepish pull to a bevy of shelter-cairns on its upper edge from where there is a fine prospect across Ribblesdale to Pen-y-ghent and Fountains Fell. Continue along a constructed path, rising in two geological 'steps' formed by the outcropping Yoredale Facies that give Ingleborough its distinctive profile, to gain the edge of the summit plateau. The summit shelter and triangulation pillar are not instantly visible, but soon come into view, along with Whernside, which together with Pen-y-ghent and Ingleborough make up the Yorkshire 'Three Peaks'.

The highest point, the true summit, is marked by a cairn on a rocky plinth a few metres north west of the triangulation pillar, and overlooks the Doe Valley. This has a history of its own, being the site of a round tower (a hospice) built in 1830, but substantially destroyed on the day of its opening by

Pen-y-ghent from Sulber

Ingleborough hillfort The top of Ingleborough holds the remains of a hillfort, with a massive encircling wall, now collapsed, around the edge of a summit plateau, also containing the foundations, still traceable in the peaty summit, of 19 circular huts believed to be a settlement of the first Iron Age man in this district. It was from this elevated vantage point, named Rigodunum, that the Brigantian leader, Venutius, led a revolt against the Romans which was not finally quelled until AD74, by Julius Agricola.

participants rather the worse for drink: the curved stones which formed its base are still clearly seen.

The onward descent leaves the north east corner of the summit plateau to gain a path along the southern flank of Simon Fell to a derelict shooting hut **C**. Beyond lies a weird landscape known as Sulber Scars, a massive desert of fissured white limestone through which a path picks its way to a lonely signpost at SD 777 734. Horton-in-Ribblesdale lies not far ahead, but here the route turns right on a grassy path to reach a stile at Sulber Gate **D**.

Continue ahead, keeping the wall on the left and when the path forks at a cairn a short distance farther on, keep right, making for the conspicuous cairn atop Long Scar. Later, before reaching Long Scar, another cairn marks a change of direction, again right, to enter a wide grassy amphitheatre known as Clapham Bottoms. The path is clear enough and leads via one gate to another at the head of Long Lane **E**, an old bridleway connecting Clapham and Selside in Ribblesdale.

A short way down Long Lane there is a fine view of Trow Gill, its naked limestone walls contrasting with the moulded grassy slopes of glacial moraine to its right. There are splendid views, too, across woodlands below in which shelters the village of Clapham, while a conspicuous dip in the lane marks the line of the North Craven Fault.

Long Lane eventually meets Thwaites Lane at a T-junction. Turn right into Thwaites Lane and descend towards Clapham, passing through two tunnels built by the Farrers to protect the privacy of their estate. This tunnelled lane ends near Clapham church at the top end of the village, from where the car park lies only a short distance away to the left. ●

Gunnerside, Kisdon and Muker

walk 28

Start
Gunnerside

Distance
11¼ miles (18km)

Height gain
1,790 feet (545m)

Approximate time
6 hours

Route terrain
Mainly farmland; upland moors; riverside paths; road walking

Parking
Parking area at Gunnerside

OS maps
Landranger 92 (Barnard Castle & Richmond) and 98 (Wensleydale & Upper Wharfedale), Explorer OL30 (Yorkshire Dales – Northern & Central area)

GPS waypoints
SD 951 982
Ⓐ SD 910 986
Ⓑ NY 895 011
Ⓒ SD 903 985
Ⓓ SD 933 978

Linking three of Upper Swaledale's delightful villages, this walk, even the longer version, is easy and most agreeable. With the River Swale as a near constant companion, the route explores one of the most outstanding regions of the Dales. This is a walk of magnificent views and great variety embracing riverside meadows, hills, woods, waterfalls and a taste of the Pennine Way long-distance trail.

Gunnerside The village of Gunnerside dates from the time the dale was settled by the Vikings; its name derives from 'Gunner's saetr', meaning 'Gunner's dwelling place'. In the 19th century, the village was at the epicentre of an important lead mining industry largely concentrated in Gunnerside Gill to the north of the village, which still bears the scars and remains of this industry. Today, it enjoys all the appeal of typical Dales settlements: attractive stone cottages clustered around a village square and from which they radiate; its position just above the Swale is exquisite, perched comfortably amid a complex landscape.

The first part of the walk follows a surfaced lane and makes for speedy and easy progress with lovely views across the dale. Leave the village by setting off along the middle one of three possible lanes branching left from the apex of the bend in the main valley road as it passes through Gunnerside, and follow the lane across the edge of the moors as at first it climbs above the dale, and then steadily descends to the tiny village of Ivelet.

Where the lane meets Shore Gill, it descends to cross it and then rises on the other side to a road junction. Here, bear right, climbing for a while before levelling off and starting to descend to Calvert Houses.

On approaching the first buildings at Calvert, take the track that passes behind them, continuing as the dale starts to change direction a little. Above Rampsholme Farm, the lane ceases to be surfaced, and here two tracks continue forward. Take the right-hand track, and when this forks a short distance farther on, branch left on the more prominent track Ⓐ, now following this as the route heads northwards into upper Swaledale. *Down below, to the left, Rampsholme Bridge spans the river, and anyone preferring to take the shorter option, should here leave the main track and double back down to the bridge – but do not* cross it. *The return leg, which takes a low-level route past the bridge, is described below.*

Now simply follow the delightful track up the dale towards the V-shaped ravine of Swinner Gill. The path rises steadily before dropping to cross the gill. Beyond, the track now climbs steeply, passing below delightfully named Crackpot Hall, and soon starting to descend as it races on above the spectacular Kisdon Force to intercept the Pennine Way **B**: a short stretch here is also part of the Northern Coast to Coast Walk, so the bridge spanning the Swale (just before which there are some lovely low waterfalls) is quite a meeting of ways.

Go down to the Swale bridge and climb the rising path on the other side. At the top, turn sharply left to join the southbound Pennine Way, which is now followed across the occasionally rugged flanks of Kisdon Hill. Throughout, the scenery is outstanding and leads to an impressive view over the village of Muker down the length of Swaledale.

At an obvious path junction **C**, bear left

onto an enclosed track that zigzags downwards to Muker. On entering the village bear left, and left again at a footpath sign for Gunnerside and Keld, crossing a stone stile and then on a partially paved path across a succession of fields that in spring are bright with buttercups and lead to the bridge spanning the Swale. Cross the bridge and immediately turn right onto a low-level path for Gunnerside. *Here the description for the shorter alternative continues.*

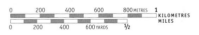
River Swale above Muker

The path leads to a gated gap-stile near a barn beyond which a green track runs across riverside meadows and through more gap stiles (some of them rather narrow) to reach Ivelet Bridge **D**, a lovely, single-arched construction that lies on the old corpse road linking the upper dale settlements with Grinton, at that time the nearest place with consecrated ground.

From the bridge, walk up into the village and turn right at the telephone box onto a minor road that quickly leads to a gravel path near a cottage on the left and a barn on the right. From a waymark, descend a narrow path on the right to a footbridge spanning Shore Gill. Now another agreeable trail of meadows and stiles leads back to Gunnerside. On the approach to Gunnerside, ignore paths leading down to the riverbank, and branch left instead to a gated gap-stile and a green path across fields back to Gunnerside, finally reached through a small estate of stone-built houses. ●

SCALE 1:25 000 or 2½ INCHES to 1 MILE *4CM to 1KM*

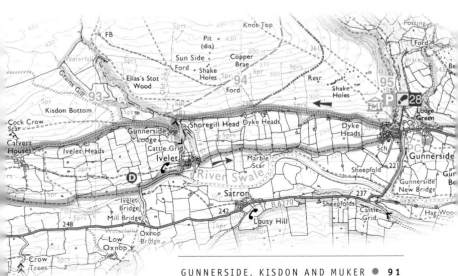

Further Information

 Safety on the Hills

The hills, mountains and moorlands of Britain, though of modest height compared with those in many other countries, need to be treated with respect. Friendly and inviting in good weather, they can quickly be transformed into wet, misty, windswept and potentially dangerous areas of wilderness in bad weather. Even on an outwardly fine and settled summer day, conditions can rapidly deteriorate at high altitudes and, in winter, even more so.

Therefore it is advisable always to take both warm and waterproof clothing, sufficient nourishing food, a hot drink, first-aid kit, torch and whistle. Wear suitable footwear, such as strong walking boots or shoes that give a good grip over rocky terrain and on slippery slopes. Try to obtain a local weather forecast and bear it in mind before you start. Do not be afraid to abandon your proposed route and return to your starting point in the event of a sudden and unexpected deterioration in the weather. Do not go alone and allow enough time to finish the walk well before nightfall.

Most of the walks described in this book do not venture into remote wilderness areas and will be safe to do, given due care and respect, at any time of year in all but the most unreasonable weather. Indeed, a crisp, fine winter day often provides perfect walking conditions, with firm ground underfoot and a clarity that is not possible to achieve in the other seasons of the year. A few walks, however, are suitable only for reasonably fit and experienced hill walkers able to use a compass and should definitely not be tackled by anyone else during the winter months or in bad weather, especially high winds and mist. These are indicated in the general description that precedes each of the walks.

 Walkers and the Law

The Countryside and Rights of Way Act (CRoW Act 2000) extends the rights of access previously enjoyed by walkers in England and Wales. Implementation of these rights began on 19 September 2004. The Act amends existing legislation and for the first time provides access on foot to certain types of land – defined as mountain, moor, heath, down and registered common land.

Where You Can Go
Rights of Way
Prior to the introduction of the CRoW Act, walkers could legally access the countryside only along public rights of way. These are either 'footpaths' (for walkers only) or 'bridleways' (for walkers, riders on horseback and pedal cyclists). A third category called 'Byways open to all traffic' (BOATs), is used by motorised vehicles as well as those using non-mechanised transport. Mainly they are green lanes, farm and estate roads, although occasionally they will be found crossing mountainous area.

Rights of way are marked on Ordnance Survey maps. Look for the green broken lines on the Explorer maps, or the red dashed lines on Landranger maps.

The term 'right of way' means exactly what it says. It gives a right of passage over what, for the most part, is private land. Under pre-CRoW legislation walkers were required to keep to the line of the right of way and not stray onto land on either side. If you did inadvertently wander off the right of way, either because of faulty map reading or because the route was not clearly indicated on the ground, you were technically trespassing.

Local authorities have a legal obligation to ensure that rights of way are kept clear and free of obstruction, and are signposted where they leave metalled roads. The duty of local authorities to install signposts extends to the placing of signs along a path or way, but only where the authority considers it necessary to have a signpost or waymark to assist persons unfamiliar with the locality.

The New Access Rights
Access Land
As well as being able to walk on existing rights of way, under the new legislation you now have access to large areas of open land. You can of course continue to use rights of way footpaths to cross this land, but the main difference is that you can now lawfully leave the path and wander at will, but only in areas designated as access land.

Where to Walk
Areas now covered by the new access rights – Access Land – are shown on Ordnance Survey Explorer maps bearing the access land symbol on the front cover.

'Access Land' is shown on Ordnance Survey maps by a light yellow tint surrounded by a pale orange border. New orange coloured 'i' symbols on the maps will show the location of permanent access information boards installed by the access authorities.

Restrictions
The right to walk on access land may lawfully be restricted by landowners, but whatever restrictions are put into place on access land they have no effect on existing rights of way, and you can continue to walk on them.

Dogs
Dogs can be taken on access land, but must be kept on leads of two metres or less between 1 March and 31 July, and at all times where they are near livestock. In addition land-owners may impose a ban on all dogs from fields where lambing takes place for up to six weeks in any year. Dogs may be banned from moorland used for grouse shooting and breeding for up to five years.

General Obstructions
Obstructions can sometimes cause a problem on a walk and the most common of these is where the path across a field has been ploughed over. It is legal for a farmer to plough up a path provided that it is restored within two weeks. This does not always happen and you are faced with the dilemma of following the line of the path, even if this means treading on crops, or walking round the edge of the field. Although the latter course of action seems the most sensible, it does mean that you would be trespassing.

Other obstructions can vary from overhanging vegetation to wire fences across the path, locked gates or even a cattle feeder on the path.

Use common sense. If you can get round the obstruction without causing damage, do so. Otherwise only remove as much of the obstruction as is necessary to secure passage.

If the right of way is blocked and cannot be followed, there is a long-standing view that in such circumstances there is a right to deviate, but this cannot wholly be relied on. Although it is accepted in law that highways (and that includes rights of way) are for the public service, and if the usual track is impassable, it is for the general good that people should be entitled to pass into another line. However, this should not be taken as indicating a right to deviate whenever a way is impassable. If in doubt, retreat.

Report obstructions to the local authority and/or the Ramblers.

 Useful Organisations

Council for National Parks
6-7 Barnard Mews, London SW11 1QU
Tel. 020 7924 4077
www.cnp.org.uk

The Yorkshire Dales National Park Authority
Colvend, Grassington, Skipton, North Yorkshire BD23 5LB
Tel. 01756 751600
www.yorkshiredales.org.uk
Yoredale, Bainbridge, Leyburn, North Yorkshire DL8 3EL
Tel. 01969 652300

National Park Authority Visitor Centres:
Aysgarth Falls: 01969 662910
Grassington: 01756 751690

Hawes: 01969 666210
Malham: 01729 833200
Reeth: 01748 884059

Campaign to Protect Rural England
128 Southwark Street,
London SE1 0SW
Tel. 020 7981 2800
www.cpre.org.uk

Forestry Commission
Silvan House, 231 Corstorphine Road,
Edinburgh EH12 7AT
Tel. 0131 334 0303
www.forestry.gov.uk

Long Distance Walkers' Association
www.ldwa.org.uk

National Trust
Membership and general enquiries:
PO Box 39, Warrington WA5 7WD
Tel. 0844 800 1895
www.nationaltrust.org.uk

Natural England
Northminster House,
Peterborough PE1 1UA
Tel. 0845 600 3078
www.naturalengland.org.uk

Yorkshire and The Humber Regional Offices:
Northallerton Tel. 0300 060 3788
York Tel. 0300 060 1911

Ordnance Survey
Tel. 08456 05 05 05
www.ordnancesurvey.org.uk

Ramblers
Tel. 020 7339 8500
www.ramblers.org.uk

Yorkshire Tourist Board
www.yorkshire.com

Local tourist information offices:
Bedale: 01677 424604
Horton in Ribblesdale: 01729 860333
Ingleton: 015242 41049
Leyburn: 01748 828747

Pateley Bridge: 01423 711147
Richmond: 01748 828742
Settle: 01729 825192
Skipton: 01756 792809

Youth Hostels Association
Trevelyan House, Dimple Road,
Matlock, Derbyshire DE4 3YH
Tel. 0800 0191 700 (General enquiries)
www.yha.org.uk

 ## Ordnance Survey maps of the Yorkshire Dales

The Yorkshire Dales are covered by Ordnance Survey 1:50 000 (1¼ inches to 1 mile or 2cm to 1km) scale Landranger map sheets 92, 97, 98, 99 and 104. These all-purpose maps are packed with information to help you explore the area. Viewpoints, picnic sites, places of interest and caravan and camping sites are shown, as well as public rights of way information such as footpaths and bridleways.

To examine the Yorkshire Dales in more detail, and especially if you are planning walks, Explorer maps OL2 (Yorkshire Dales – Southern & Western areas), OL19 (Howgill Fells & Upper Eden Valley), OL30 (Yorkshire Dales – Northern & Central areas) and OL41 (Forest of Bowland & Ribblesdale) at 1:25 000 (2½ inches to 1 mile or 4cm to 1km) are ideal.

Other Explorer maps covering the area are:

298 (Nidderdale)

302 (Northallerton & Thirsk)

304 (Darlington & Richmond)

To get to the Yorkshire Dales, use Ordnance Survey OS Travel Map-Route Great Britain at 1:625 000 (1 inch to 10 miles or 4cm to 25km) scale or Ordnance Survey Road Travel Map 4 (Northern England) at 1:250 000 (1 inch to 4 miles or 1cm to 2.5km) scale.

Ordnance Survey maps and guides are available from most booksellers, stationers and newsagents

Text:	Terry Marsh
	Introduction, Brian Conduit
Photography:	Terry Marsh
Editorial:	Ark Creative (UK) Ltd
Design:	Ark Creative (UK) Ltd

© Crimson Publishing, a division of Crimson Business Ltd

 This product includes mapping data licensed from Ordnance Survey® with the permission of the Controller of Her Majesty's Stationery Office. © Crown Copyright 2011. All rights reserved. Licence number 150002047. Ordnance Survey, the OS symbol and Pathfinder are registered trademarks and Explorer, Landranger and Outdoor Leisure are trademarks of the Ordnance Survey, the national mapping agency of Great Britain.

ISBN: 978-1-85458-680-3

While every care has been taken to ensure the accuracy of the route directions, the publishers cannot accept responsibility for errors or omissions, or for changes in details given. The countryside is not static: hedges and fences can be removed, stiles become gates, field boundaries can alter, footpaths can be rerouted and changes in ownership can result in the closure or diversion of some concessionary paths. Also, paths that are easy and pleasant for walking in fine conditions may become slippery, muddy and difficult in wet weather, while stepping stones across rivers and streams may become impassable.

If you find an inaccuracy in either the text or maps, please write to Crimson Publishing at the address below.

First published 1989 by Jarrold Publishing
Revised and reprinted 1990, 1991, 1993, 1995, 1997, 1999, 2002, 2004, 2005, 2007, 2008, 2010, 2011.

This edition first published in Great Britain 2011 by Crimson Publishing, a division of:
Crimson Business Ltd,
Westminster House, Kew Road, Richmond, Surrey, TW9 2ND

www.totalwalking.co.uk

Printed in Singapore. 14/11

All rights reserved. No part of this publication may be reproduced, transmitted in any form or by any means, or stored in a retrieval system without either the prior written permission of the publisher, or in the case of reprographic reproduction a licence issued in accordance with the terms and licences issued by the CLA Ltd.

A catalogue record for this book is available from the British Library.

Front cover: Striding along the Pennine Way, Horton-in-Ribblesdale
Page 1: Heading for Whernside

Unearth *The best of* Britain series
from Crimson Publishing

Accessible, contemporary guides by local experts

The best of Britain series includes...

**Norfolk and
Suffolk**

**The Lake
District**

**Isle of Wight
and the
New Forest**

**Northern
Ireland**

Devon

Cotswolds

**Edinburgh and
East Coast
Scotland**

**Cornwall and
the Isles of
Scilly**

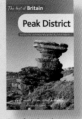

Peak District

Easy to navigate...informative and packed with practical information - *Which? Holiday*

crimson   www.crimsonpublishing.co.uk